T0135076

Advanced Information and Knowledge Processing

Information systems and intelligent knowledge processing are playing an increasing role in business, science and technology. Recently, advanced information systems have evolved to facilitate the co-evolution of human and information networks within communities. These advanced information systems use various paradigms including artificial intelligence, knowledge management, and neural science as well as conventional information processing paradigms.

The aim of this series is to publish books on new designs and applications of advanced information and knowledge processing paradigms in areas including but not limited to aviation, business, security, education, engineering, health, management, and science.

Books in the series should have a strong focus on information processing - preferably combined with, or extended by, new results from adjacent sciences. Proposals for research monographs, reference books, coherently integrated multi-author edited books, and handbooks will be considered for the series and each proposal will be reviewed by the Series Editors, with additional reviews from the editorial board and independent reviewers where appropriate. Titles published within the Advanced Information and Knowledge Processing Series are included in Thomson Reuters' Book Citation Index and Scopus.

More information about this series at http://www.springer.com/series/4738

Tankiso Moloi · Tshilidzi Marwala

Artificial Intelligence in Economics and Finance Theories

Tankiso Moloi
School of Accounting
University of Johannesburg
Johannesburg, South Africa

Tshilidzi Marwala
University of Johannesburg
Johannesburg, South Africa

ISSN 1610-3947 ISSN 2197-8441 (electronic)
Advanced Information and Knowledge Processing
ISBN 978-3-030-42964-5 ISBN 978-3-030-42962-1 (eBook)
https://doi.org/10.1007/978-3-030-42962-1

This Springer imprint is published by the registered company Springer Nature Switzerland AG
The registered company address is: Gewerbestrasse 11, 6330 Cham, Switzerland

Preface

Literature has not attempted to utilize advances in technology to modernize economics and finance theories that are fundamental in the decision-making process for the purpose of allocating scarce resources among other things. *Artificial Intelligence in Finance and Economics Theories* describes what Artificial Intelligence is and how it is changing the field of finance and economics, particularly some of the key theories embedded in this field.

Following the introductory chapter, the book discusses the impact of Artificial Intelligence in the Solow Growth Theory, the Ricardian Theory, the Dual-Sector Theory, the Dynamic Inconsistent Theory; the Phillips Curve, the Laffer Curve, the Adverse Selection Theory, the Moral Hazard Theory; the Creative Destruction Theory, the Agency Theory, and the Legitimacy Theory and the Legitimacy Gap.

This book is an interesting reference for graduate students, researchers, economists, policymakers and artificial intelligence practitioners with interest in finance and economic theories and artificial intelligence.

Johannesburg, South Africa
March 2020

Tankiso Moloi, Ph.D.
Professor of Accounting

Tshilidzi Marwala, Ph.D.
Professor and Vice Chancellor

Acknowledgment We want to thank the anonymous peer reviewers of this work. We further want to Dr. O. Iredele, Dr. M. Salawu, Dr. V. Denhere and Dr. D. Mhlanga, who are post-doctoral research fellows in the School of Accounting for their assistance with gathering literature in some of the theories considered.

Contents

Chapter 1
Introduction to Artificial Intelligence in Economics and Finance Theories

1.1 Introduction

The world is changing rapidly. There is no time in history when virtually every aspect, whether human life, economies or politics among other things, has been affected by the rapid change brought through by developments in information technology (Harari 2018). Technological advances have allowed humanity to discover powerful energy sources, discover faster modes of transportation for humans, goods and services, improved the speed in which we communicate, landed human beings to the moon, and there is even an attempt to send a spacecraft on a mission to the sun. Technology has allowed human beings to have a better mode of diagnosing and even curing diseases. The speed to which the COVID-19 test was developed and deployed to deal with the pandemic that engulfed the globe in the first quarter of 2020 is testimony to this. Agricultural yields have also seen an improvement, owing to technological advances. In a sense, advances in technology have enabled humanity to conquer the barriers of nature. Life has certainly improved compared to our ancestors.

In order to understand and contextualize these technological advances, Marwala and Hurwitz (2017) posit that the developments in information technology could be best characterized by the four phases of revolution in human history, namely, the first, second, third and fourth industrial revolutions (Ashton 1948; Baten 2016). Accordingly, the first industrial revolution brought mechanical innovations with the development of the steam engine, which was the key to the then industrial revolution. It was catalyzed by the scientific revolution of Isaac Newton, Robert Hooke and James Watt. The second industrial revolution started in the second half of the nineteenth century. It brought the oil-powered internal combustion engine, electricity, electric motors and electrical communication. There were major technological advances during this period, including the telephone, light bulbs, phonograph, the assembly line and mass production of goods and services.

The third industrial revolution or digital revolution came in the 1950s; it brought computerization, which included the mainframe computers, personal computers

T. Moloi and T. Marwala, *Artificial Intelligence in Economics and Finance Theories*, Advanced Information and Knowledge Processing,
https://doi.org/10.1007/978-3-030-42962-1_1

(PCs) and the Internet, and the information and communication technology (ICT) that we continue to use today. This industrial revolution was catalyzed by the invention of the transistor. The period is characterized by the advancement of technology from analog electronic and mechanical devices to the digital technology (Agrawal et al. 2018; Marwala and Hurwitz 2017).

The fourth industrial revolution arrived at the beginning of the twenty-first century. This revolution brought with it the advent of cyber-physical systems, which represent a new way in which technology becomes embedded within societies, i.e. business, government, civil society, etc., and the human body. Further, it is driven by the rapid convergence of advanced technologies across the biological, physical and digital worlds. The fourth industrial revolution is manifested by emerging technology breakthroughs in a number of fields, which include, among others, robotics, AI, biotechnology, 3D printing, advanced materials such as graphene, "Internet of Things (IoT)" and blockchain (Harari 2018; Agrawal et al. 2018; Marwala and Hurwitz 2017).

Looking at these revolutions, it is clear that they have had unique impacts on every aspect of human life, including business. Of interest though is that literature has not attempted to utilize these advances in technology to modernize economics and finance theories that are fundamental in the decision-making process for the purpose of allocating scarce resources among other things. With the simulated intelligence in machines, which allows machines to act like humans and to some extent even anticipate events better than humans, thanks to their ability to handle massive data sets, this book uses artificial intelligence to explain what these economics and finance theories mean in the context of an agent wanting to make a decision.

It is apparent that in the fourth industrial revolution, technology in general will continue to have an unprecedented role. Marwala and Hurwitz (2017) support this view; however, within the technology space, they specifically single out AI. They argue that the fourth industrial revolution is embedded on AI. Perhaps the reason they would have adopted this stance is that, nowadays, AI is everywhere. Agrawal et al. (2018) point out that AI is in "our phones, cars, shopping experiences, romantic matchmaking, hospitals, banks and all over in the media".

1.2 Artificial Intelligence

Artificial intelligence is a technique that is used to make computers intelligent (Marwala 2007, 2009). There are three types of artificial intelligence, and these are machine learning, computational intelligence and soft computing (Marwala 2009). Computational intelligence is the use of intelligent biological systems such as the flocking of birds or the colony of ants to build intelligent machines. Computational intelligence has been used successfully to create systems such as Google Maps that identify the shortest distances between two points (Marwala 2012). For an example, a population of ants, shown in Fig. 1.1, is able to build complicated anthills, shown in Fig. 1.2. What sort of economics have these ants imagined in order to be able to build

Fig. 1.1 Ants, which are able to build complicated structures such as the one illustrated in Fig. 1.2

Fig. 1.2 An anthill built by ants, such as the ones illustrated in Fig. 1.1

assets such as these? These ants have two mechanisms of building such a complicated economy, and these are: group intelligence and individual intelligence. In essence, what this means is that on its own (individual intelligence), the ant will struggle to put together such a structure, but collectively these ants are able to put together this complicated economy. This book studies how the rise of artificial intelligence would impact the economics and finance theories.

Soft computing does not require large amounts of data to train (Marwala and Lagazio 2011). One example of soft computing is fuzzy logic. Fuzzy logic uses possibility rather than probability models to create an inference system. Fuzzy logic is able to model difficult variables, such as linguistic variables. Fuzzy logic has been used to model many complex systems, including financial instruments (Patel and Marwala 2006).

Machine learning is the statistical approach to making intelligent machines. One example of machine learning is a neural network. Neural network is based on the functioning of the human brain through neurons and how they fire electrical signals to transmit information. An illustration of a neural network is shown in Fig. 1.3. It is worth noting that neural networks have been successful in modelling complex systems (Marwala 2018).

An example of machine learning is deep learning, which requires huge amounts of data to train (Leke and Marwala 2019). It is called deep learning because it has many hidden layers. Deep learning has been very successful for problems such as face recognition and voice recognition. For instance, deep learning is used when a person loads photos on Facebook, and this application automatically identifies and labels the names of the people on the photos. Because deep learning depends so much on data, it is making data emerge as the most valuable commodity, thereby arguably surpassing oil.

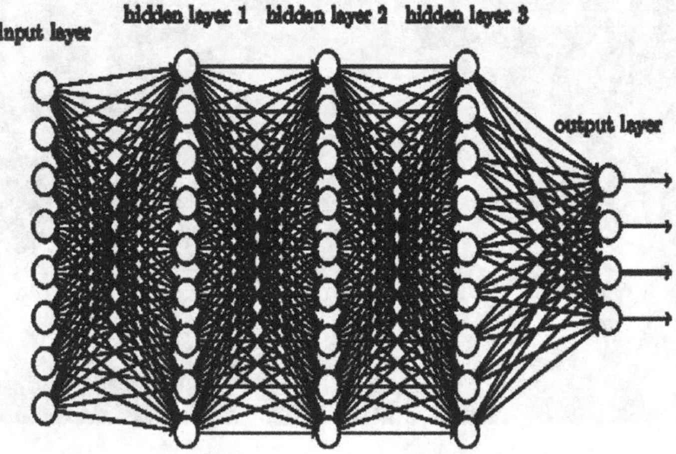

Fig. 1.3 An example of a deep neural network

It has been established that artificial intelligence can be used effectively as a prediction tool. In their attempt to clear future uncertainties so that sound decisions can be made, agents use predictions as an input into the decision-making process, where economics and finance theories would have provided a framework in which agents make decisions on how to allocate scarce resources (Marwala 2013, 2014, 2015).

As AI seizes all aspects of human life, there is a fundamental shift in the way in which humans are thinking of and doing things. Ordinarily, humans have relied on economics and finance theories to make sense of, and predict, concepts such as comparative advantage, long-run economic growth, lack or distortion of information and failures, role of labour as a factor of production and the decision-making process for the purpose of allocating resources among other theories.

The main feature of these theories is that they try to eliminate the effects of uncertainties by attempting to bring the future to the present. The fundamentals of this statement are deeply rooted in risk and risk management. Standard number 31000 of the International Standardisation Organisation (ISO) defines risk as "the effect of uncertainty on the objective". In other words, uncertainties are the main component of the deviations from the expected outcomes (Moloi 2016).

In behavioural sciences, economics as a discipline has always provided a well-established foundation for understanding uncertainties and what this means for decision-making (Agrawal et al. 2018). Economics has done this through different models that attempt to predict the future. On its part, risk management attempts to hedge or mitigate these uncertainties in order for "the planner" to reach the favourable outcome.

As explained earlier, the main feature of economic theories is that they try to eliminate the effects of uncertainties by attempting to bring the future to the present. Agrawal et al. (2018) have argued that AI (at least as it is right now) "does not actually bring us intelligence, but a critical component of intelligence—prediction". This is what humans have in the past deployed economics and financial theories to do.

With AI providing us with a critical component of intelligence, the manner in which economics and finance theories have been presented is impacted. This book focuses on how artificial intelligence is to redefine certain important economics and financial theories that, for a number of years have specifically been used for the purpose of eliminating uncertainties to allow agents to make informed decisions.

1.3 Finance and Economics

Society has evolved over the years, and one of the most interesting inventions is money. Money was invented somewhere in the Middle East. When society moved to the agricultural age, there was a problem that agricultural production was not consistent and, therefore, there was need to store food for the times of drought. The place where this storage happened was in the churches. The priests received food to store and in exchange gave a token (money). Societies are organized along the lines of money. The whole class system was fundamentally about money. The exchange of goods and services, usually using money, is what we call the economy. The dynamics of money in society is what we call finance. On understanding the economy and money, various models and theories were developed. Many of these models were not universally accepted, and, sometimes, schools of thoughts evolved along political ideological lines. In the United States, the Republicans and the Democrats are divided along the economic line. The democrats believe in what is called the demand-side economics where an economy can be stimulated to encourage aggregate demand. This is what Adam Smith called the invisible hand (Smith 2015). The Republicans, on the other hand, believe in the supply-side economics where they believe in deregulation and a limited hand in the economy; in other words, Republicans advocate for lesser government intervention in the economy.

Several theories emerged and Marwala and Hurwitz's (2017) study was on how these theories are influenced by the advances in AI. For example, they studied the laws of demand and supply and observed that advances in AI are making the principles of demand and supply more individualized, leading to individualized pricing (Mankiw and Taylor 2011). They also studied the theory of rational expectations, which prescribes that on predicting the future, agents are not systematically wrong (Muth 1961). Marwala and Hurwitz (2017) observed that the advances of AI make the theory of rational expectations more valid. When rational agents operate in the market, they do so in order to maximize their utility. The economic theory on the maximization of utility is called rational choice. Rational choice is based on the philosophical concept called utilitarianism (Friedman 1996; Mill 2001). Research has shown that it is impossible for agents to be rational. The best agents can do is to be bounded rationally. Marwala and Hurwitz (2017) observed that AI and related technologies make the bounds of rationality flexible. It turns out that if such agents are people, they never maximize utility because doing so is a risky strategy and people have evolved to be risk averse. This is called prospect theory (Kahneman and Tversky 1979). Marwala and Hurwitz (2017) observed that the bounds of rationality are better off when agents are machines than when agents are human beings.

Another economic theory is information asymmetry. Information asymmetry is a situation where the buyers and sellers of goods have unequal information (Stigler 1961; Spence 1973; Aboody and Lev 2000). In such a situation, the markets are inefficient. Marwala and Hurwitz (2017) have observed that the use of AI makes the markets more symmetrical and, therefore, improves market efficiency. Game theory is a mathematical technique that is used to understand the dynamics of a situation where agents interact. In game theory, agents interact under certain rules until they reach the Nash equilibrium (Osborne and Rubinstein 1994). Unfortunately, the mathematics works well for interactions with fewer agents. AI is able to expand the number of agents that can interact in a simulation. The reverse of game theory is called mechanism design. While in game theory, we study the interactions of agents under some set of rules until they achieve Nash equilibrium (Nash 1950), in mechanism design we have agents and know the desired Nash equilibrium and all we want to identify are the rules that will make that possible (Myerson and Satterthwaite 1983). Mechanism design has been used for market design, incentive design and in the kidney exchange market. Marwala and Hurwitz (2017) used AI to implement mechanism design.

Portfolio theory is a process of pooling financial assets together to minimize risk (Markowitz 1952). How these assets are pooled together is an optimization problem. Markowitz (1952) proposed a model that works well for stationary environments. Marwala and Hurwitz (2017) proposed the use of AI for portfolio optimization in a non-stationary environment. AI makes markets efficient, thereby improving the validity of the efficient market hypothesis (Fama 1996, 2008). This book extends the impact of AI in economics and finance to the theories that are described in the themes of the book presented below.

1.4 Themes of the Book

Chapter 2 of this book examines the Solow Theory (Solow 1956; Swan 1956). The theory postulates that growth of per-capita output is the result of capital accumulation and/or technological progress. In essence, what it says is that as the economy reaches its steady state (equilibrium), per-capita output growth is only possible through the technological progress, taking into account that technological progress is exogenous in the model. This chapter examines the tenets of the Solow Theory, focusing on the main assumptions and how the theory is applied in economics. The manner in which the application of AI would affect assumptions and how the theory is applied are also discussed. Conclusions are drawn on how the theory could be modernized, given the effect of AI.

Chapter 3 looks at the Ricardian Theory (Dornbusch et al. 1977). The theory assumed two countries, producing two goods that are homogeneous across countries and firms within an industry. In this theory, labour is the main factor of production, mobile within the country's industries but cannot move abroad. Labour is also homogeneous within a country; however, this may be different across countries. The implication of homogeneous labour within a country with differences between countries implies that the production technology could be different between two trading nations. Technological advances have turned the world into a global village. In essence, the borders have essentially been flattened. AI will change the very nature of the Ricardian Theory in the sense that, as it evolves, AI flattens the borders and possibly reduces reliance on labour. For instance, one information technology specialist can give guidance on how the application works over the Internet from wherever they are in the world; doctors can perform virtual life-saving operations, and professors now can give virtual classes.

Chapter 4 pays attention to the Dual-Sector economic theory. At a high level, this theory supposes that the economy can be divided into two parts: the developed and the underdeveloped. In the two sectors, labour can be migrated from the underdeveloped sector to the developed sector until it makes no more economic sense to do so, and this is called the Lewis turning point. In the era of AI, this framework can be used to study the migration of labour from humans to machines until it makes no-sense to continue doing so, thereby reaching the Lewis-Automation turning point.

Chapter 5 looks at the Dynamic Inconsistency theory, which reflects a changing nature of human beings' preferences over time that could result in these preferences differing at some point in the preference continuum, yielding the inconsistencies. This means that not all selected preferences are aligned, and that there is a misalignment somewhere in the preference continuum (Simaan and Cruz 1973). With the ability to store the information, learn about the previous behaviour of the agent and possibly pre-empt the next move that the agent is likely to take, while also providing basket options, AI would awaken the subconscious mind of the agent, challenging the notion of Dynamic Inconsistency with that of an informed choice.

Chapter 6 is dedicated to the Phillips Curve. This theory states that inflation and unemployment have a stable and inverse relationship (Phillips 1958). In this theory, economic growth is expected to generate inflation and more work opportunities, which decreases unemployment. This chapter examines these tenets, focusing on the main assumptions. The manner in which the application of AI would impact on these assumptions and the potential impact of AI on this theory are discussed. In particular, our focus is on employment. In the automated world, economic growth could be fuelled by robotic infrastructure. Because individuals would possibly have been replaced by the robotic infrastructure, growth would not be accompanied by employment opportunities. At the same time, since this could result in unemployment, the demand for goods and services could be expected to be put under pressure. If supply remains the same because robotic infrastructure will be producing potentially at a higher rate than humans, prices could be expected to decline, dampening inflation prospects.

Chapter 7 looks at the Laffer Curve (Gahvari 1989). It examines the tenets of the Laffer Curve, which defines the relationship between tax revenue and the tax rate. We study the impact of the advances in automation and its impact on tax collection. In particular, we study how advances in AI are changing the very nature of the Laffer Curve.

Chapter 8 attends to the theory of Adverse Selection. Economics, risk management and insurance are disciplines that employ both the concepts of moral hazard and adverse selection (Akerlof 1970). Adverse selection occurs when one agent in a transaction has more information than the other party, thus enjoying an advantage. Since most information in a market-driven economy is transmitted through pricing, adverse selection will result in unfair pricing of goods and services and the unfair advantage on the part of the agent with more information. This chapter examines how the Adverse Selection theory will look like in a situation where the information is digitally and easily accessible by all parties in the transaction. The modern world is highly characterized by digitization, which ensures access to more information about the counterparty in the transaction. This will change the very nature of the Adverse Selection theory.

Chapter 9 focuses on the Moral Hazard theory (Arrow 1963). Moral hazard occurs when the agent behaves in a manner that they would not have behaved had they not put mitigating circumstances in place. In insurance contracts, for instance, an agent would put themselves in a risky situation because they know that they are insured. This exposes the insurer. Alternatively, in financing transactions, one agent would not enter into the contract in good faith, i.e. they would have provided misleading information about its assets, liabilities or credit-bearing capacity. Similar to the Adverse Selection theory, this chapter examines how the Moral Hazard theory changes in a situation where the information is digitally and easily accessible by all parties in the transaction. The modern world is highly characterized by digitization, which ensures access to more information about the counterparty in the transaction. This changes the very nature of the Adverse Selection theory.

Chapter 10 examines the Creative Destruction Theory (Reinert and Reinert 2006). This theory was derived from the work of Karl Marx by Joseph Schumpeter. As technology improves, a "gale of creative destruction" is unleashed through the process of industrial mutation, where the economic structure is revolutionized without much intervention of the external forces. In the process of this revolution, old technologies are destroyed and new ones are created. We examine whether the creative destruction is a result of human inefficiencies, for instance, the lack of data, the inability to store crucial data, the inability to get insights on the data so as to learn about the previous behaviour of the agent and which of these factors hinders the owners of the destructed technology to pre-empt the next move that the agent is likely to take, while also providing basket options so that their technology remains relevant and moves with time. With the ability to store the information, learn about the previous behaviour of the agent and possibly pre-empt the next move that the agent is likely to take, while also providing basket options, AI would provide current technology holders with vital intelligence to remain competitive, relevant and timely, thus challenging the notion of Creative Destruction as it is presented with that of the Creative Modernisation.

Chapter 11 examines the Agency Theory. The Agency theory was developed by Jensen and Meckling (1976). According To Kopp (2019), the agency theory is a principle utilized in an attempt to explain the complex relationship that exists between the owners (principal) and managers (agents) of the business. Jensen and Meckling (1976) define the agency relationship as a form of contract between a company's owners and its managers, where the owners (as principal) appoint an agent (the managers) to manage the company on their behalf. This relationship is most commonly found between shareholders as principals and company executives as agents. Other similar relationships are found between financial planners and portfolio managers acting as agents on behalf of their clients, the investors, acting as principals, and a lessee acting as an agent on behalf of the lessor, and the property owner acting as the principal among others.

Chapter 12 examines the Legitimacy. Theory and the Legitimacy Gap. According to Guthrie and Ward (2006), the Legitimacy theory is derived from the concept of organizational legitimacy. Legitimacy is considered by Suchman (1995) as a generalized perception that the actions of an organisation are desirable and appropriate within some socially constructed system of norms, values, beliefs and definitions.

Chapter 13 provides a synopsis of each theory that was considered.

1.5 Key Points

Advances in technology have enabled humanity to conquer the barriers of nature. Life has certainly improved compared to our ancestors.

- Existing literature has not attempted to utilize advances in technology to modernize economics and finance theories that are fundamental in the decision-making process for the purpose of allocating scarce resources among other things. The main feature of economic theories is that they try to eliminate the effects of uncertainties by attempting to bring the future to the present.
- As AI provides us with a critical component of intelligence, the manner in which economics and finance theories have been presented will be impacted. This book focuses on how artificial intelligence redefines certain important economics and financial theories that are used for purposes of eliminating uncertainties so as to allow agents to make informed decisions.
- With the simulated intelligence in machines, which allows machines to act like humans and, to some extent, even anticipate events better than humans, thanks to their ability to handle massive data sets, this book uses artificial intelligence to explain what these economics and financial theories mean in the context of the agent wanting to make a decision.

References

Aboody D, Lev B (2000) Information asymmetry, R&D, and insider gains. J Financ 55(6):2747–2766

Agrawal A, Gans J, Goldfarb A (2018) Prediction machines: the simple economics of artificial intelligence. Harvard Business Review Press

Akerlof GA (1970) The market for 'memons': quality uncertainty and the market mechanism. Q J Econ 84(3):488–500

Arrow K (1963) Uncertainty and the welfare economics of medical care. Am Econ Rev 53(5):941–973

Ashton TS (1948) The industrial revolution (1760–1830). Oxford University Press, Oxford

Baten J (2016) A history of the global economy: from 1500 to the present. Cambridge University Press, Cambridge

Dornbusch R, Fischer S, Samuelson P (1977) Comparative advantage, trade and payments in a Ricardian Model with a Continuum of Goods. Am Econ Rev 67(5):823–839

Fama EFK (1996) Multifactor explanation of asset pricing anomalies. Journal of Finance 51(1):55–84. https://doi.org/10.1111/j.1540-6261.1996.tb05202.x

Fama EFK (2008) Dissecting anomalies. J Financ 63(4):1653–1678. https://doi.org/10.1111/j.1540-6261.2008.01371.x.F

Friedman J (1996) The rational choice controversy. Yale University Press, New Haven

Gahvari F (1989) The nature of government expenditures and the shape of the Laffer curve. J Public Econ 40(2):251–260

Harari YN (2018) 21 Lessons for the 21st century. Jonathan Cape, London

Jensen MC, Meckling WH (1976) Theory of the firm: managerial behavior, agency costs and ownership structure. In: Jensen MC (ed) A theory of the firm: governance, residual claims and organizational forms (December 2000). Harvard University Press. Available at SSRN https://ssrn.com/abstract=94043 or http://dx.doi.org/10.2139/ssrn.94043 (Journal of Financial Economics (JFE), Vol. 3, No. 4, 1976)

Kopp CM (2019) Agency theory. Available from https://www.investopedia.com/terms/a/agencytheory.asp

Kahneman D, Tversky A (1979) Prospect theory: an analysis of decision under risk. Econometrica 47(2):263

Leke CA, Marwala T (2019) Deep learning and missing data in engineering systems. Springer, London

Mankiw NG, Taylor MP (2011) Economics (2nd ed, revised ed). Cengage Learning, Andover

Markowitz HM (1952) Portfolio Selection. J Financ 7(1):77–91

Marwala T (2018) Handbook of machine learning: foundation of artificial intelligence. World Scientific Publication

Marwala T, Hurwitz E (2017) Artificial intelligence and economic theory: skynet in the market. Springer International Publishing

Marwala T (2015) Causality, correlation, and artificial intelligence for rational decision making. World Scientific, Singapore

Marwala T (2014) Artificial intelligence techniques for rational decision making. Springer, Heidelberg

Marwala T (2013) Economic modeling using artificial intelligence methods. Springer, Heidelberg

Marwala T (2012) Condition monitoring using computational intelligence methods. Springer, Heidelberg

Marwala T, Lagazio M (2011) Militarized conflict modeling using computational intelligence. Springer, Translated into Chinese by the National Defence Industry Press, Heidelberg

Marwala T (2009) Computational intelligence for missing data imputation, estimation, and management: knowledge optimization techniques. IGI Global, PA

Marwala T (2007) Computational intelligence for modelling complex systems. Research India Publications, Delhi

Mill JS (2001) Utilitarianism and the 1868 speech on capital punishment. Hackett Publishing Company, Indianapolis/Cambridge

Moloi T (2016) A cross sectoral comparison of risk management practices in South African organizations. Probl Perspect Manag 14(3):99–106

Muth JF (1961) Rational expectations and the theory of price movements. Econometrica 29(3):315–335

Myerson RB, Satterthwaite MA (1983) Efficient mechanisms for bilateral trading. J Econ Theory 29(2):265–281

Nash J (1950) Equilibrium points in n-person games. Proc Natl Acad Sci 36(1):48–49

Osborne MJ, Rubinstein A (1994) A course in game theory. MIT Press, Boston, MA

Patel P, Marwala T (2006) Neural networks, fuzzy inference systems and adaptive-neuro fuzzy inference systems for financial decision making. Lecture notes in computer science, vol 4234. Springer, Berlin, Heidelberg, pp 430–439

Phillips AW (1958) The relation between unemployment and the rate of change of money wage rates in the United Kingdom, 1861–1957. Economica New Ser 25(100):283–299

Reinert H, Reinert ES (2006) Creative destruction in economics: Nietzsche, Sombart, Schumpeter. Eur Herit Econ Soc Sci 3:55–85

Simaan M, Cruz JB Jr (1973) On the stackelberg strategy in nonzero-sum games. J Optim Theory Appl 11(5):533–555

Smith A (2015) The wealth of nations: a translation into modern English. Industrial systems research, Machester, England

Solow RM (1956) A contribution to the theory of economic growth. Q J Econ 70(1):65–94

Spence M (1973) Job market signaling. Q J Econ 87(3):355–374. MIT Press
Stigler GJ (1961) The economics of information. J Polit Econ 69(3):213–225
Suchman M (1995) Managing legitimacy: strategic and institutional approaches. Acad Manag Rev 20(3):571–611
Swan TW (1956) Economic growth and capital accumulation. Econ Rec 32(2):334–361

Chapter 2
The Growth Model

2.1 Introduction

This chapter examines the Solow theory (Solow 1956). The theory postulates that the growth of per-capita output is the result of capital accumulation and technological progress. In essence, what it says is that as the economy reaches its steady state (equilibrium), per-capita output growth is only possible through technological advancement, taking into account that technological progress is exogenous in the model. In this chapter, we examine the tenets of the Solow theory, focusing on the main assumptions and how the theory is applied. The manner in which the application of AI would affect the theory's assumptions is discussed. We present our conclusions on how the theory will be affected given the effect of AI.

The Solow model has made a substantial contribution to our quest to understand the underlying factors that determine economic growth in different countries. It emerged as a response to the Harrod–Domar model that sought to emphasize how growth could go hand-in-hand with increasing unemployment, seen as potential dysfunctional aspects of growth. Solow tried to demonstrate, through the growth model, why the Harrod–Domar model was not an appropriate place to begin discussing the phenomenon dubbed potential dysfunctional aspects of growth.

The growth model explains long-run economic growth by taking into account factors of production that determine growth rate for different countries, which factors include capital accumulation, labour or population growth (also known as technological progress). In developing the long-run economic growth, Solow ignored certain aspects; for instance, the short-run fluctuations in employment and savings rates. Perhaps Solow did this to avoid complicating the model; hence, his emphasis on long-run economic growth. This eclectic approach is common among macroeconomists, where models are often developed to help explain one particular aspect of macroeconomy.[1]

[1] https://www.tcd.ie/Economics/staff/whelanka/topic1.pdf.

T. Moloi and T. Marwala, *Artificial Intelligence in Economics and Finance Theories*, Advanced Information and Knowledge Processing,
https://doi.org/10.1007/978-3-030-42962-1_2

2.2 The Catching-Up Growth Phenomenon

The Solow model argues that a sustained rise in capital investment increases the growth rate only temporarily. The main cause of the temporary growth is the ratio of capital to that of labour increases. However, the marginal product of additional units of capital may decline (hence the diminishing returns). When this happens, the economy will move back to a long-term growth path, with the real gross domestic product (GDP) growing at the same rate as the growth of the workforce plus a factor to reflect improving productivity.

In the growth model, as countries continue to inject additional capital and labour into the market, and as they continue to formulate fresh ideas and innovate, growth will follow (Solow 1956). In explaining the role of the first two factors of production, namely, capital and labour, the theory argues that the ability to grow the economy by merely injecting additional inputs of capital and labour into the system would normally work in the context of the catching-up growth.

The catching-up growth would continue until such a stage where the economy is, to a considerable extent, grown and caught up with peer economies in certain developmental aspects. If, for instance, Lesotho was left behind on a particular developmental perspective by a peer country such as eSwatini, injecting capital and labour into the Lesotho system would be expected to work. Lesotho and eSwatini were selected as our example because they share common characteristics of development. They are both in the Southern African region, both landlocked by South Africa, both have a monarchy system of governance, and have small population sizes.

The catching-up growth phenomenon is often used in the explanation of high economic growth recorded in certain underdeveloped countries compared to their developing counterparts as a way of closing the gap between these two, and in the description of high economic growth registered in certain developing countries compared to their developed counterparts as a natural law of catching up with a richer country. The high growth levels would often happen because of a higher marginal rate of return on invested capital in faster growing countries.

The state of the economy would be presented by the basic Solow model as follows:

$$Y_t = F(K_t, L_t) \tag{2.1}$$

where Y is the *output*, K *capital* and L *labour*.

2.3 The Steady Growth Path Phenomenon

At some point, the economic response that underdeveloped, developing and developed countries will get from injecting additional capital and labour into the system does not necessarily move these economies to the next level of growth as output per-capita remains constant. In this regard, the economies would now be trapped into and

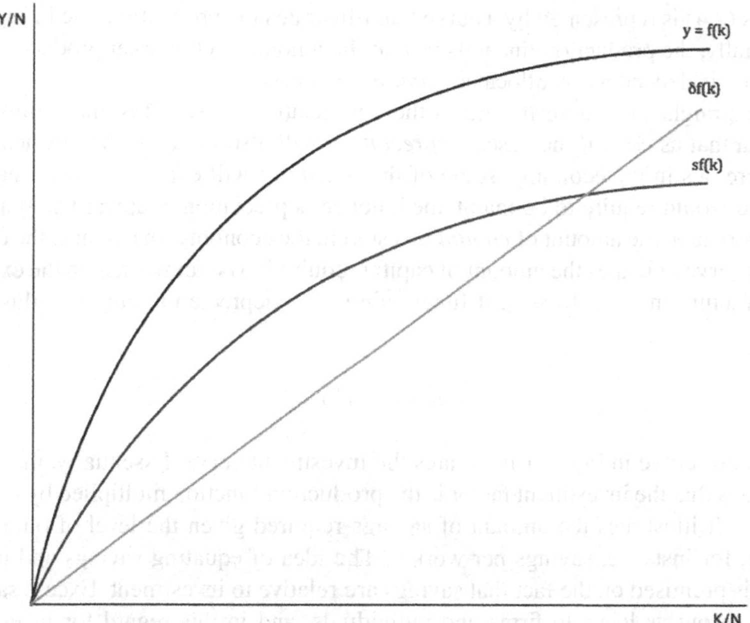

Fig. 2.1 The steady growth state

remain in the steady growth state (Romer 2006); for example, a steady-state growth path would have been reached when output, capital and labour are all growing at the same rate. This is when output per worker and capital per worker are constant. Figure 2.1 describes the steady-state growth path.

Figure 2.1 illustrates the steady growth state of the economy. The horizontal line represents the amount of *capital* available in the economy, and N is the overall amount of people in the workforce (*labour*). Both the amount of capital available in the economy and the overall amount of people in the workforce can be illustrated in formulae as follows:

$$k = K/N \tag{2.2}$$

The vertical line represents the overall *output* in the economy and *N* is the overall amount of people in the workforce (*labour*). This can be illustrated as follows:

$$y = Y/N \tag{2.3}$$

Given (2.2) and (2.3) above, (2.1) can be rewritten as follows:

$$y = f(k) \tag{2.4}$$

This (2.4) is represented by a curve that illustrates the production line in Fig. 2.1. Essentially, the production line tells us that the amount each worker produces in the economy is dependent on allocated *capital* per worker.

The straight-line curve illustrates the depreciation curve. This curve illustrates the idea that as *capital* increases, *depreciation* will also increase. As physical capital increases in the economy, some of the machines will experience the wear and tear and would require to be maintained, hence depreciation is upward sloping and proportional to the amount of *capital* invested in the economy. In essence, the depreciation curve indicates the amount of capital required to be reinvested on the existing infrastructure in order to keep it functioning. The depreciation curve is illustrated by:

$$d = \delta f(k) \tag{2.5}$$

The last curve in Fig. 2.1 illustrates the investment curve. Essentially, this curve illustrates that the investment factor is the production function multiplied by the saving rate. It illustrates the amount of savings required given the level of output per worker, for instance, savings per worker. The idea of equating savings and investments is premised on the fact that savings are relative to investment. Excess savings are given out as loans to firms and individuals, and in this regard for investment purposes. Based on this discussion, it is clear that we can determine the amount of investment per worker that is re-injected into the economy. By determining this, with this curve, we can further determine the amount of new capital that is re-injected into the economy:

$$i = s * f(k) \tag{2.6}$$

Looking at Fig. 2.1, just below the level where the depreciation curve intersects the investment curve, it is clear that the levels of investments are higher than the depreciation required to maintain the infrastructure. The excess investments that are not used to maintain the existing infrastructure are utilized to increase capital infrastructure, thus stimulating the output per worker. At the level above the intersection of the depreciation curve and the investment curve, it becomes clear that the levels of investments are lower than the depreciation required to maintain the existing infrastructure. In this regard, there is a shortage of investments required to maintain the existing infrastructure. No new capital infrastructure will be undertaken; thus, the output per worker will decline. As these forces continue to pull on one side and push to the other side, the economy will always end up in the steady-state equilibrium, which is a point where the depreciation curve and the investment curve intersect in Fig. 2.1. At the point of intersection, whatever excess investment is available is just sufficient to maintain the existing infrastructure. Nothing can be reinvested to stimulate the economy and take it out of the trap.

2.4 The Cutting Edge Growth Path

To kick start the growth process by unleashing the growth potential requires economies to formulate fresh ideas and innovate. Innovation and formulation of new ideas is done in order to prevent the economy from being caught in the steady growth state (Barro and Salai-Martin 2004). As new ideas and innovations propel the economy to the next level, that economy would have shifted its economic growth strategies and employed the cutting edge growth strategies. The application of cutting edge growth strategies is mostly applied in developed countries. In some cases, however, cutting edge growth strategies do get applied in some of the developing countries.

The state of the economy would be presented by the basic Solow growth model as follows:

$$Y_t = F\left(A_t, K_t, L_t\right) \quad (2.7)$$

where Y is the *output*, *A ideas leading to innovation*, *K capital* and *L labour.* In our formulae above, ideas are utilized in an innovative way and on an ongoing basis in order to transform both the physical and human capitals during the production process, which would consistently ensure that production yields improve. In this case, the economy will avoid being-trapped into a steady state. Therefore, the growth model implies that the long-run improvement in the standard of the living would depend on the economy's fundamental characteristics, such as the population growth rate, the savings rate, the rate of technical progress and the rate of capital depreciation (Liu 2007).

2.5 Artificial Intelligence and the Growth Model

In the era of artificial intelligence, where a huge part of the production line is expected to be automated (mechanized), the Solow growth theory is impacted. Marwala (2007, 2009) have defined Artificial intelligence as a technique that is used to make computers intelligent. Accordingly, intelligent machines have a capability to process huge amounts of data, whether in a structured or unstructured format. The Institute of Chartered Accountants of England and Wales (2018) has argued that intelligent machines could process this data far much more than humans ever would. What makes intelligent machines more suitable for production floors is the fact that they can pick up weaker or more complex patterns in data than we can (The Institute of Chartered Accountants of England and Wales 2018). As such, intelligent machines may be better in environments that we find less predictable.

One other advantage of intelligent machines in the context of the production floor is that they can be far more consistent decision-makers. They do not suffer from tiredness or boredom (The Institute of Chartered Accountants of England and Wales 2018), which could be fatal in hazardous environments such as mining and quarrying.

Given this discussion, in a closed economy such as the one discussed above, the production line curve in Fig. 2.1, about which the earlier discussion indicated that the amount each worker produces in the economy is dependent on allocated *capital* per worker, is to be impacted by the automation. In automation, the amount that each robotic infrastructure or a programme produces in the economy will be dependent on allocated *capital* per robot.

Interestingly, depending on how this is to be classified, two things could happen. The first case scenario could include a condition where the classifications are left as they are. In this case, the robotic infrastructure or programmes replace part of or all labour, resulting in the situation where theory is revised to indicate that the amount that each robotic infrastructure or a programme produces in the economy will be dependent on allocated *capital* per robot (and/or partially labour).

The second scenario could include a condition where the robotic infrastructure or programme is seen as part of the capital. In these conditions, the straight-line curve that illustrates the depreciation curve could be expected to be steeper. As *capital* would have increased with the procurement of robotic infrastructure and/or programmes to enhance the existing infrastructure, *depreciation* will also increase twofold. As physical capital increases in the economy, some of the machines and robotic infrastructure will experience wear and tear, and would require to be maintained. The effect of this, however, is likely to be balanced by higher output volumes per robot, given the fact that machines do not go on strike or lunch.

Assuming that there will still be savings and demand, Fig. 2.1 would initially demonstrate an investment curve that will be higher than the depreciation curve. In this regard, the levels of investments will be higher than the depreciation required to maintain the infrastructure. The excess investments that will not be used to maintain the existing infrastructure will be utilized to increase capital infrastructure further, thus stimulating the output robot (and partially per worker, depending on the level of automation).

As the physical capital ages, there will slowly be a reversal of the initial achievements. This is demonstrated in Fig. 2.1 by any level that is above a point of intersection of the depreciation curve and the investment curve. To explain this point, we revisit the full or partial replacement of labour by robotic infrastructure and programmes. In this regard, total/partial labour will be out of work, and it will not be in a position to save, pay taxes or demand goods that will massively be produced by the automated manufacturing factories. In this scenario, since there are no excess funds to save, investments on the new capital infrastructure will shrink. The levels of investments will be lower than the depreciation required even to maintain the existing infrastructure. No new capital infrastructure will be undertaken. Hence, the output per robotic infrastructure will eventually decline.

In the steady state, we explained that as forces continue to pull on one side and push to the other side, in the long run, the economy will end up in the steady-state equilibrium, which is a point where the depreciation curve and the investment curve intersect as shown in Fig. 2.1.

In the revisited scenario painted above, where the total/partial labour could be out of work because of automation, it should be expected that this cohort will be unable to save, pay taxes or demand goods that will massively be produced by the automated manufacturing factories, there would not be investments to stimulate the economy and take it out of the trap. The economy will be in a long-run economic crisis.

2.6 Key Points

- The growth model explains long-run economic growth by taking into account factors of production that determine growth rates for different countries. The factors include capital accumulation, labour or population growth (also known as technological progress).
- In the era of artificial intelligence, where a huge part of the production line is expected to be automated, the Solow growth theory is impacted.
- Intelligent machines impact the production floor for the reason that they have capability to process huge amounts of data, whether in a structured or unstructured format. This data could be processed far much more than that humans ever would.
- What makes intelligent machines more suitable for production floors is the fact that they can pick up weaker or more complex patterns in data than we can. As such, intelligent machines may be better in environments that we find less predictable.
- One other advantage of intelligent machines in the context of the production floor is that they can be far more consistent decision-makers. They do not suffer from tiredness or boredom, which could be fatal in hazardous environments such as mining and quarrying.
- There are two scenarios that could play out. The first scenario includes a condition where the classifications are left as they are. In this case, the robotic infrastructure or programme replaces part of or all labour, resulting in the situation where theory is revised to indicate that the amount that each robotic infrastructure or a programme produces in the economy will be dependent on allocated capital per robot (and/or partially labour).
- The second scenario could include a condition where the robotic infrastructure or programme is seen as part of the capital. In these conditions, the straight-line curve that illustrates the depreciation curve could be expected to be steeper. Further, since total/partial labour will be out of work, it will not be in a position to save, pay taxes or demand goods that will massively be produced by the automated manufacturing factories. In this scenario, since there are no excess funds to save, investments to the new capital infrastructure will shrink. The levels of investments will be lower than the depreciation required even to maintain the existing infrastructure. No new capital infrastructure will be undertaken. Thus the output per robotic infrastructure will eventually decline.
- If these formulated scenarios play themselves out, the long-run steady state is potentially replaced by the long-run economic crisis.

References

Barro RJ, Salai-Martin X (2004) Growth models with exogenous saving rates (The Solow-Swan Model): economic growth, 2nd edn. MIT University Press, Cambridge, MA

Liu D (2007) Growth theory and application: the case of South Africa. Working Paper: 2007–14, University of Pretoria

Marwala T (2007) Computational intelligence for modelling complex systems. Research India Publications, Delhi

Marwala T (2009) Computational intelligence for missing data imputation, estimation, and management: knowledge optimization techniques. IGI Global, PA

Romer D (2006) The solow growth model: advanced macroeconomics, 3rd edn. McGraw–Hill, New York

Solow RM (1956) Contribution to the theory of economic growth. Q J Econ 70(1):65–94

The Institute of Chartered Accountants of England and Wales (2018) Artificial intelligence and the future of accountancy. ICAEW Thought Leadership, IT Faculty, UK

Chapter 3
Comparative Advantage

3.1 Introduction

Primarily, there exist five reasons countries would want to trade with other countries (also known as international trade) (McKenzie 1954; Jones 1961; Samuelson 2001). Firstly, international trade takes place because countries would have advanced differently in the technological space. These differences in technology would permit the country that is advanced in that particular technology to hold an advantage of some sort compared to the chosen trading partners.

Secondly, international trade would take place between countries because of the differences in resource endowments. Different countries have different resource bases. Whatever one country has as a resource is used in that country, and the excess is exported to a different country that is in need of that resource. Exports provide the country with foreign currencies that it requires in order to import goods or services that it lacks. For instance, South Africa has significant proven reserves of the platinum resource. Platinum is used in catalytic converters for motor vehicles (Hobson 2018). In this regard, South Africa will use whatever amount of platinum it requires for its domestic market, and the excess will be sold to the export market, which earns South Africa foreign currencies.

Based on its geological advantages, South Africa holds the advantage over its trading partners in the platinum market. In this scenario, we assume that there is no substitute or the substitute is unreliable or is expensive. This would be a similar case in significant oil-producing countries such as the Kingdom of Saudi Arabia and other members of the Organisation of Oil Exporting Countries (OPEC) (Colgan 2014).

Thirdly, due to culture and other related factors, demand and preferences would differ between countries. On this basis, we expect that different countries would have different preferences or demands for various products. For instance, maize (corn) is a staple food for most South Africans. Generally, South Africans use corn to make "pap" (porridge) (Isaacson 2005). Thus, even if the price is the same, South Africans, in all likelihood, are expected to demand more maize (corn) than their counterparts,

T. Moloi and T. Marwala, *Artificial Intelligence in Economics and Finance Theories*, Advanced Information and Knowledge Processing,
https://doi.org/10.1007/978-3-030-42962-1_3

such as India where the expectation would be that there will be more demand for rice.

Fourthly, in a country such as China, for instance, where more than a billion tons of steel products are produced and made available to the market at a cheaper price, the presence of economies of scale generates advantageous trade for China since excess production could be exported to other countries cheaper (Ashby and Jones 1992). An excellent example of this is the comparison of the domestic market price of steel in South Africa and the imported price of steel from China by South African steel users (Steyn 2016).

Finally, sometimes, the countries' policies could tip the scale resulting in prices of goods or services under consideration altered. In this regard, the levying of taxes on certain products or the subsidization of the product could cause an alteration in the prices levied, giving price advantage or disadvantage to the participating country. The policy alteration means that a profitable trade would have arisen solely based on policy differences across the trading countries. The assumption here is that the product that is in question could be found somewhere else. If the product is a natural resource that is only available in some areas of the world, this assumption may not hold.

As an instance of the above, recently, the United States of America (USA) and the People's Republic of China (PRC) were engaged in a tit-for-tat tariff imposition against each other's products. BBC (2020) reports that with this policy, the USA aimed to encourage consumers to buy American products by making imported goods more expensive. Table 3.1 demonstrates that the USA imposed tariffs to cause an alteration in the prices levied in an attempt to get price advantage and discourage PRC imports. The PRC responded to roll-back the impact on its economy.

From our discussion of five reasons for the existence of international trade, it is clear that it will be a long call to expect that a single trade model could be designed.

Table 3.1 Policy alteration: USA versus PRC

Time	USA policy alteration	US tariffs	PRC response to policy alteration
July 2018	USD 34b worth of PRC's products	25%	USD 34b worth of USA products
August 2018	USD 16b worth of PRC's products	25%	USD 60b worth of USA products
September 2018	USD 200b worth of PRC's products	10%	USD 60b worth of USA products
May 2019	USD 200b worth of PRC's products	25%	N/A
June 2019	N/A	N/A	USD 60b worth of USA products
August 2019	USD 112b worth of PRC's products (stage 4a)	15%	

Source BBC (2020) and Tax Foundation (2020)

Further, it will be a long call to expect that any designed single trade model could comprehensively incorporate all the five reasons for the existence of international trade within its parameters. As observed in the Solow–Swan Theory, models are often developed to help explain one particular aspect of the macroeconomy. The Ricardian Theory (comparative advantage) follows the same eclectic approach, which was highlighted as a standard approach among macroeconomists in their attempt to avoid complications by including more variables in theory (Wood 1991; Davis 1995). The eclectic approach, therefore, is often selected to try to simplify the phenomenon.

In order to make things easy and more understandable so that a particular point could be emphasized and attended to without causing complications, economists would attempt to simplify the world by choosing a model that generally contains one reason or the other. In this regard, the Ricardian Theory focuses on international trade, particularly the comparative advantage that one country could derive by focusing on specific aspects of production where its processes are more efficient.

The emergence of various theories that seek to address similar phenomenon suggests that even though they may have selected to focus on a certain phenomenon, economists do not necessarily believe that one theory or model is a sufficient tool to be utilized in order to explain all possible outcomes. Instead, what we are learning from the emergence of various theories that seek to address similar phenomenon, albeit in a different form, is that we must try to understand the world by looking at what a collection of different models tells us about the same phenomenon.

According to Deardorff (2007), the Ricardian Theory is arguably the earliest model of trade to have appeared in the writings of classical economists. For Deardorff (2007), it is probably the last surviving theory that is still acceptable and considered useful today as it is a common trend to feature this theory in the first few chapters of most textbooks that focus on international economics, where the principles of comparative advantage would be introduced. In essence, most trade economists concur that the Ricardian Theory offers some of the most compelling reasons supporting international trade.

This is to say that should country A be in a position produce a particular product in an efficient manner that lowers the cost of production of such a product, at the same time, a trading partner, called country B is also able to produce a different product in an efficient manner which lowers the cost of production of that particular product, and both these products are needed in both these countries, it is logical that country A and country B should trade with each other as they both stand to gain from such a transaction. The trade between these two countries will primarily be focusing on exporting a good that they each produce cheaper and importing a good that will cost each more to produce. Perhaps this is what obligated Deardorff (2007) to declare that this theory is still acceptable and still considered useful today.

This chapter looks at what will happen to the theory of comparative advantage in the light of the advances in the fourth industrial revolution. To understand the fourth industrial revolution, one needs to understand the first, second and third industrial revolutions (Horn et al. 2010). The first industrial revolution was driven by mechanical energy, and it gave us the steam engine and revolutionized production. The second industrial revolution was driven by electricity and an electric motor, and brought the assembly line. The third industrial revolution was driven by semi-conductor devices and gave us the digital revolution. We are now living in what is called the fourth industrial revolution, and it will merge the physical, biological and digital systems into one system (Schwab 2017). It is driven by technology, such as artificial intelligence, robotics and 3D printing among others.

Artificial intelligence is a computational technique for building machines that are intelligent (Marwala 2018). It has been used successfully to model complex problems such as HIV (Marwala 2007), to make decisions with missing information (Marwala 2009; Leke and Marwala 2019), to model mechanical machines (Marwala 2010; Marwala et al. 2017), to understand interstate conflict (Marwala and Lagazio 2011), for detection of faults in mechanical and electrical structures (Marwala 2013), to model economic and financial systems (Marwala 2013; Marwala and Hurwitz 2017), in crowdsourcing (Xing and Marwala 2018a), in robotics (Xing and Marwala 2018b) and to in model causality (Marwala 2014, 2015). There are various types of artificial intelligence, and these include soft computing, evolutionary algorithms and machine learning. Machine learning uses statistics, whereas soft computing uses fuzzy logic, rough sets, etc. and evolutionary algorithms use principles of evolution and behaviour of social systems to build intelligent machines. Within machine learning, there are algorithms such as neural networks. Neural networks with many layers are called deep learning.

3.2 Assumptions of the Ricardian Theory

According to Ruffin (2002), in working on determining comparative advantage between two countries, David Ricardo's original model had focussed primarily on the amount of labour used to produce traded goods in order to compare the relative advantages of the countries involved (Ricardo 1917). Ruffin (2002) indicates that the constructs of the model first appeared in 1844.

In reality, the world is a complicated place that does not only consist of two countries. Many factors account for the differences; it is not only technology as assumed by the theory of comparative advantage. We do not have countries that are only producing two goods; there are a variety of countries producing a variety of products.

In its emphasis on labour, the theory of comparative advantage assumes that labour is fixed. We know that in reality, this cannot be the case. Still on labour, the theory of comparative advantage emphasizes full employment, which means that labour is unable to immediately and costlessly move to other industries.

Labour is further seen as identical. Identical labour will effectively mean that you could move an employee from a mining and quarrying industry to the higher education and training industry. Accordingly, as these employees get to a new industry, they would immediately be as productive as the labour that was already in the higher education and training industry. These assumptions make the Ricardian Theory more of a thought experiment.

3.3 The Concept of Opportunity Cost and Comparative Advantage

For us to understand the Ricardian theory, two concepts need to be distilled, and these are the opportunity costs and the comparative advantage concepts. Opportunity costs are opportunities forgone in order to make a choice. For example, suppose John has to choose to either go to Cape Town or New York for a holiday. If he chooses to go to Cape Town, then he forgoes going to New York and, therefore, going to New York is the opportunity cost. The problem with the concept of opportunity costs is that for any choice that one makes, there are many other choices (opportunity costs) that a person could have made (von Wieser 1927).

The concept of comparative advantage is rooted in the notion of comparing. This concept comes to economics in various forms. For example, in economics, there is a concept called rational choice. Suppose Lusani has $100 and she needs to invest it. Suppose she considers three scenarios, the first one to go to Monte Casino and gamble in the hope of making $1 million. The second scenario is to invest it in the stock market with the hope of making $1000. The third scenario is to put it in the bank, and she is guaranteed to make $10. What option should she take and what criteria should she use to make such a choice?

The idea of comparing these three options is so that the agent can choose the best option. In rational choice, this will be an option that will result in the most significant gain. Friedman (1996) refers to this maximization of utility as the art of evaluating the comparative advantage of each option (Friedman 1996). In essence, in comparative advantage, one is comparing the advantages of each option (Findlay 1987).

Through the concepts of opportunity cost and comparative advantage, the Ricardian Theory emphasizes the point that should country A be in a position produce specific products in an efficient manner which lowers the cost of production of such a product, and at the same time, a trading partner, called country B, is also able to produce a different product in an efficient manner which lowers the cost of production of that particular product, and both these products are needed in both these countries, it is logical that country A and country B should trade with each other as they both stand to gain from such a transaction. In this example, both countries would be faced with a trade-off situation, such as whether to use the resources at their disposal to produce certain products and forego other products. In this regard, the opportunity cost for country A measures the cost of not producing something else they may have produced. Say, in deciding to employ all the resources at its disposal to mine more iron ore and ship (export) it in its original form rather than beneficiating it downstream, South Africa is forfeiting the opportunity to produce steel. The opportunity cost of mining iron ore and railing it on the export channel through Saldanha Bay to foreign clients is the tons of steel not going through the blast furnace. A trade-off that South Africa faces is how much of the iron ore it should mine and export, or how much steel it should produce, given the resource constraints.

In our example including South Africa, the country will have a comparative advantage in mining iron ore and exporting it through the iron ore export channel in Saldanha Bay if the opportunity cost of mining iron ore is lower compared to the trading partner's, in this regard, China. In terms of the Ricardian Theory, South Africa has a comparative advantage in mining and exporting iron ore to its trading partners if it can utilize its resources most efficiently when it mines iron ore compared to when it produces steel, which it could in turn import at a reasonable price from its trading partner, China.

3.4 Artificial Intelligence and the Ricardian Theory

Earlier, we highlighted the fact that the Ricardian Theory puts more emphasis on labour. We emphasized the point that there are other factors of production besides labour that are employed in the production of goods. We further pointed out that in its emphasis on labour, the Ricardian Theory assumes that labour is fixed, which we know, in reality, cannot be the case. In fact, with advances in artificial intelligence and robotics, labour is increasingly migrating from humans to machines.

Still on labour, we pointed out that the Ricardian Theory emphasizes full employment, which means that labour is unable to immediately and costlessly move to other industries. In its emphasis of labour, we pointed the fact that the Ricardian Theory views labour as identical across indutries and disciplines, which would effectively mean that you could move an employee from a mining and quarrying industry to the higher education and training industry, and, as they get there, these employees would hit the ground running and be as productive as the labour that was already in the higher education and training industry. In reality, this cannot hold as labour would require new training and build new skills in order for it to be effective in its new tasks. Be that as it may, in this section, we examine the effect of artificial intelligence on labour; the main factor of production emphasized by the Ricardian Theory.

3.5 Artificial Intelligence and the Assumption that Labour Cannot Migrate

On the assumption that labour is fixed and cannot migrate beyond borders, it is worth noting that technology has made the world a global village. The ever-increasing connectivity provided by real-time information, coupled with the rise of professional networking services and platforms such as LinkedIn (business and employment-oriented service) is likely going to permit that work is allocated and possibly done digitally (Weiner 2014). This reduces business expenses associated with office space, water and electricity (Moloi 2018).

AI will change the very nature of the Ricardian Theory in the sense that, as it evolves, it flattens the borders and possibly reduces reliance on labour. For instance, one Information Technology (IT) specialist can give guidance on how the application works over the Internet while based somewhere in the world. Several other specialists can give services virtually. These specialists need not move abroad, and possibly, no assistants (i.e. assistant professor/markers) will be required in the performance of these functions.

3.6 Artificial Intelligence and the Assumption of Full Employment as Well as the Immobility of Labour

Much as there is no economy that could claim to have generated full employment, which has its own challenges for the Ricardian Theory, it is now well accepted that the majority of repetitive jobs are going to be impacted as they can be done by computer programmes or robots, which will further challenge the Ricardian assumption of full employment. In an era that is slowly moving towards intense automation, the apprehension is about the loss of jobs, especially for those that have not improved their skill set in order to continue to the relevant era dominated by technology. Big debates are around how technology can be leveraged to create new opportunities and how people can be retrained to be relevant.

In the 2017 study, the McKinsey Global Institute points to the fact that intelligent agents and robots could eliminate as much as 30% (this is estimated to be 400 and 800 million jobs) of the world's human labour. The McKinsey Global Institute compares the effects that the AI scenario will have with the effects that were last seen when there was move away from agricultural labour during the 1900s in the United States and Europe (Manyika et al. 2017).

A further extension of this assumption was that labour would be unable to move to other industries immediately. As some of the industries move towards automation, remaining labour in automated industries will be expected to adapt so that it can remain competitive and relevant in the labour market, lest it runs the risk of irrelevance. The newly acquired skills could be utilized in new frontiers opened by the automated world. The Manyika et al. (2017) points out that even when some tasks are automated, employment in those occupations may not decline, but workers may perform new tasks.

In recognition of the fact that labour would need to be adaptable and gain new expertise in order to remain relevant, the 2018 World Economic Forum (WEF), the Future Jobs Report estimate that globally, machines and algorithms would create 133 million new roles; however, this will be offset by 75 million jobs expected to be displaced by 2022. This data points to the fact that there will be a net gain of 58 million jobs created by AI. Clearly, these jobs will be requiring specific skill sets that would demand that in order to survive and remain competitive and relevant, labour would have to be adaptable and gain new expertise in the new frontier driven by AI.

The examples we have provided above point to two interesting facts. These facts challenge the full employment and the immobility of labour assumptions. Our first observation is that with the full ramping up of AI, specific tasks will be affected, resulting in redundancies and possibly more unemployment should the existing labour not be ready to be absorbed by newly created industries. Our second observation is that the ramping up of AI could result in the mobility of labour. We assume here that existing labour is retrained to gain new skill sets, which will allow them to migrate from their old tasks to new tasks. Should AI create new industries, labour can migrate to these industries, which would not have existed and would apply new skills, which they would not have had.

3.7 Artificial Intelligence and the Assumption that Labour Is Identical

Earlier, we pointed out that the Ricardian Theory views labour as identical. In this regard, an example was made that this assumption implies that you could move an employee from a mining and quarrying industry to the higher education and training industry and as they get there, these employees will be instantly competent and be as productive as the labour that was already in the higher education and training industry. It was pointed out that in reality, this cannot hold as labour is dissimilar, with different skill sets, qualifications and the level of experiences.

With algorithms and machines, we will likely see a labour system integration. Earlier, we pointed out the ever-increasing connectivity provided by real-time information, coupled with the rise of professional networking services and platforms such as LinkedIn. We indicated that this is likely going to permit that work is allocated and, possibly, done digitally. Due to the systems integration, which will include, among other things, the references by previous clients on the quality of work done by an employee in the past, which information would be available to the user at the click of the button, there is a possibility of further dissimilating labour, including those that may be having similar qualifications and have the same level of experience, based, inter alia, on their previous conduct (Moloi 2018).

Integrated labour systems could do this by warranting that those that are sourced are highly sought individuals that are effective and efficient. Advantages to the highly sought employees are that businesses that are interested in expanding and improving productivity will begin to bid for these types of employees. The integrated technology will allow these highly sought employees to compare the bids. The likelihood is that they will contract with a bidder that remunerates them higher. Since the ordinary course of employment as we know it would have shifted, these highly sought people will also be in a position to hold numerous contracts as compared to holding one permanent employment. This is expected to improve their earnings.

The challenge, of course, lies with those that are not deemed highly sought, which could be condemned to the world of unemployment. The unemployed would have more reliance on government assistance. If the government revenue-generating mechanisms, such as taxation, are not adequately aligned with the developments at that stage, the government will find it challenging to raise sufficient revenue to cater for the expanding demands. We will expand on this in our discussion of the Laffer Curve.

3.8 Comparative Advantage and Automation

During the era of intense automation, the principle of "winners take all" will dominate the economy. For example, in the social networking space, there is no room for the second best to Facebook or Twitter or LinkedIn or Uber. Because of this new phenomenon, countries that will develop their sovereign economy around these technologies of the fourth industrial revolution will have to be protectionist in order to have a stake in these industries. For example, in China, Facebook, Twitter and Uber are banned (or highly regulated). It is because of this reason that China was able to create alternatives to these such as DiDi and Baidoo. Having said this, though, poor countries that rely on aid and other forms of assistance from more prosperous nations may not be in a position to take such a position. Specifically, because of this reason, we are of the view that more prosperous countries may become more protectionist and, thereby, limiting international trade.

The idea that the fourth industrial revolution brings new forms of production, such as additive manufacturing and 3D printing, means that the physical nature of a firm will change. While in the first, second and third industrial revolutions factories became more significant and more centralized, in the fourth industrial revolution factories will become smaller and distributed. The fourth industrial revolution is driven by AI, which is easy to replicate because it is software based.

Several vital questions arise: What becomes of developing countries in the trade space? What will then be the competitive edge for countries? What will be the driver of international trade if labour is no longer as necessary in production? Technology will become the sole basis for competition, but given the fact that technology is more natural to replicate, what will differentiate countries? The ability to update and generate technology, i.e. innovation, is likely going to be a competitive edge going forward. In conclusion, we are of the view that AI brings the possibility of building multiple variables models of the relationships of qualitative and quantitative data to model the Ricardian Theory.

3.9 Key Points

- The almost unrealistic and not worldly assumptions make the Ricardian Theory more of a thought experiment.

- Concerning AI and the assumption of full employment, we argue that no economy could claim to have generated full employment, which has its own challenges for the Ricardian Theory. With algorithm and machines, it is now well accepted that a majority of repetitive jobs are going to be impacted as they can be done by programmes or robots, which will further challenge the Ricardian assumption of full employment.
- Concerning AI and the immobility of labour, our view is that as some of the industries move towards automation, labour that would have been to the now automated industries will be expected to adapt so that it can remain competitive and relevant in the labour market, lest it runs the risk of irrelevance. The newly acquired skills could be utilized in new frontiers opened by the automated world.
- On AI and the assumption that labour cannot migrate, we note that the ever-increasing connectivity provided by real-time information, coupled with the rise of professional networking services and platforms such as LinkedIn (a business and employment-oriented service), is likely going to permit that work is allocated and possibly done digitally. This reduces business expenses associated with office space, water and electricity. AI will change the very nature of the Ricardian Theory in the sense that, as it evolves, it flattens borders and possibly reduces reliance on labour.
- On AI and the assumption that labour is identical, our position is that the algorithm and machines are likely going to bring along the labour system integration. These systems will permit that work is allocated and, possibly, done digitally. Due to the systems integration, which will include, among other things, references by previous clients on the quality of work done by the employee in the past, which information would be available to the user at the click of the button, there is a possibility of further dissimilating labour, including those that may be having similar qualifications and have the same level of experience, based, inter alia, on their previous conduct. The integrated technology will allow these highly sought employees to compare the bids. The likelihood is that they will contract with a bidder that remunerates them higher. Those that are not deemed highly sought could be condemned to the world of unemployment.
- Finally, we think AI brings the possibility of building multiple variables models of the relationships of qualitative and quantitative data to model the Ricardian Theory.

References

Ashby MF, Jones DRH (1992) An introduction to microstructures, processing and design. London, Butterworth-Heinemann, UK

BBC (2020) A quick guide to the US-China trade war. https://www.bbc.com/news/business-45899310. Accessed 05 February 2020

Colgan J (2014) OPEC, the phantom menace. Washington post. Accessed Retrieved 31 December 2018

Davis D (1995) Intra-industry trade: A Heckscher-Ohlin-Ricardo approach. J Int Econ 39:201–226
Deardorff AV (2007) The Ricardian model. The University of Michigan, USA
Findlay R (1987) Comparative Advantage. New Palgrave: A Dict Econ 1:514–517
Friedman J (1996) The rational choice controversy. Yale University Press, New Haven
Hobson P (2018) Currency shocks knock platinum to 10-year lows. Reuters. Accessed 31 December 201
Horn J, Rosenband L, Smith M (2010) Reconceptualizing the Industrial Revolution. MIT Press, Cambridge MA
Isaacson C (2005) The change of the staple diet of black South Africans from sorghum to maize (corn) is the cause of the epidemic of squamous carcinoma of the oesophagus. Med Hypotheses 64(3):658–660
Jones RW (1961) Comparative advantage and the theory of tariffs. Rev Econ Stud 28(3):161–175
Leke CA, Marwala T (2019) Deep learning and missing data in engineering systems. Springer, London
Manyika J, Lund S,Chui M, Bughin J, Woetzel J, Batra P, Ko R, Sangh S (2017) Jobs lost, jobs gained: what the future of work will mean for jobs, skills, and wages. McKinsey Global Institute
Marwala T (2018) Handbook of machine learning: foundation of artificial intelligence, vol 1. World Scientific Publication
Marwala T, Hurwitz E (2017) Artificial intelligence and economic theory: skynet in the market. Springer
Marwala T, Boulkaibet I, Adhikari S (2017) Probabilistic finite element model updating using bayesian statistics: applications to aeronautical and mechanical engineering. Wiley
Marwala T (2015) Causality, correlation, and artificial intelligence for rational decision making. World Scientific, Singapore
Marwala T (2014) Artificial intelligence techniques for Rational decision making. Springer, Heidelberg
Marwala T (2013) Economic modeling using artificial intelligence methods. Springer, Heidelberg
Marwala T, Lagazio M (2011) Militarized conflict modeling using computational intelligence. Springer, Heidelberg
Marwala T (2010) Finite element model updating using computational Intelligence techniques: applications to structural dynamics. Springer, Heidelberg
Marwala T (2009) Computational intelligence for missing data imputation, estimation, and management: knowledge optimization techniques. IGI Global, PA
Marwala T (2007) Computational intelligence for modelling complex systems. Research India Publications, Delhi
McKenzie LW (1954) Specialization and efficiency in world production. Rev Econ Stud 21(3):165–180
Moloi T (2018) Get ready for the fourth industrial revolution. https://www.iol.co.za/sundayindependent/analysis/get-ready-for-the-fourth-industrial-revolution-16209139. Accessed 07 January 2018
Ricardo D (1917) On the principles of Political Economy and Taxation. In Sraffa P (ed) Works and correspondence of David Ricardo, vol I. Cambridge University Press, pp 1951
Ruffin RJ (2002) David Ricardo's discovery of comparative advantage. Hist Polit Economy 34:727–748
Samuelson P (2001) A Ricardo-Sraffa paradigm comparing the gains from trade in inputs and finished goods. J Econ Lit 39(4):1204–1214
Schwab K (2017) The fourth industrial revolution. Crown Publishing Group, New York
Steyn L (2016) SA's steel industry on brink of collapse. Mail and Giuardian. Accessed 31 December 2019
Tax Foundation (2020) Tracking the economic impact of US tariffs and retaliatory actions. https://taxfoundation.org/tariffs-trump-trade-war/. Accessed 05 February 2020
von Wieser F (1927) In: Ford Hinrichs A (ed) (translator). Social economics. Adelphi, New York

Weiner J (2014) LinkedIn in China: connecting the world's professionals. Linkedin official blog. Accessed 31 December 2018
Wood JC (1991) David Ricardo: critical assessments. Routledge, London, UK
World Economic Forum (WEF) (2018) The future of jobs. Centre for the New Economy and Society, Geneva, Switzerland
Xing B, Marwala T (2018a) Smart computing applications in crowdfunding. CRC Press (Taylor and Francis), Routledge, London
Xing B, Marwala T (2018b) Smart maintenance for human–robot interaction: an intelligent search algorithmic perspective. Springer, London

Chapter 4
The Dual-Sector Model

4.1 Introduction

The dual-sector economic theory is essentially a theory of economic development. Arthur Lewis proposed it in the year 1954 in a treatise entitled "Economic development with unlimited supplies of labour" (Hall 2012). The proposition of the dual-sector model yielded the joint Nobel Prize for Economics in 1979 (Menzies 2018).

In examining Arthur Lewis' Nobel Prize's autobiography, Menzies (2018) observes that it made it clear that Arthur Lewis' interest was in the fundamental forces that determine the rate of economic growth. Accordingly, there were a varicty of models that sought to determine the rate of economic growth at that time; some of these models were at an emerging phase. As such, Arthur Lewis was of the view that his model had to divert from the mainstream models of the time.

Gollin (2014) explains that in order to divert his models from the mainstream models of the time, Arthur Lewis sought to identify a unique process of development in overpopulated countries. In the process of doing this, Arthur Lewis understood that the dual-sector economic model would not apply to the countries that had already transformed into capitalist production (Gollin 2014).

According to Pettinger (2017), the dual-sector economic model was conceptualized on the concept of a dual economy. The concept of dual economy is explained by Menzies (2018) as a concept that relies on dualism. It utilizes dualism in order to describe economies with asymmetries in production technologies.

As Hall (2012) indicates, the concept of dualism stemmed from Lewis' observation that for many developing economies, there were two different economic segments. Pettinger (2017) highlights these two segments as:

- A capitalist-based manufacturing sector—this manufacturing sector will essentially be geared to service the global markets. In other words, we think what this means is that this sector will be a source of exports for that particular country. It

T. Moloi and T. Marwala, *Artificial Intelligence in Economics and Finance Theories*, Advanced Information and Knowledge Processing,
https://doi.org/10.1007/978-3-030-42962-1_4

will earn that particular country foreign currencies that may be needed when they import products or services that they require for the domestic economy; and

- A labour-intensive agricultural sector—this agricultural sector will be characterized by low productivity and, possibly, some inefficiencies within the system, hence the low productivity. Accordingly, this sector is geared towards subsistence farming or local markets.

The section above provided a high-level introduction of the dual-sector model. We indicated that the dual-sector model pointed to two different segments of the economy that mainly describe the dual-sector model. In order to locate AI in the context of a dual-sector model, and its implications, we provide high-level details of the dual-sector model in the following few sections.

4.2 Tenets of the Dual-Sector Model

In the previous section, we introduced the concept of dualism. We highlighted that it is said to have originated from Lewis' observation that for many developing economies, there are two different economic segments, namely, a capitalist-based manufacturing sector and a labour-intensive agricultural sector. We noted that the manufacturing sector would primarily be geared to service the global markets. In our view, what this means is that this sector will be a source of exports for that particular country. Further, we pointed out that this will be a sector that will earn the particular country the much needed foreign currency for purposes of importing products or services that they require for the domestic economy. One the other hand, the labour-intensive agricultural sector will be characterized by low productivity and, our view was that it would possibly have some inefficiencies within the system and lesser deployment of machines, hence the characterization of this sector by low productivity. Accordingly, this sector is geared towards subsistence farming or local markets.

In explaining the dual-sector economic model, Pettinger (2017) postulates that Lewis propounded that in the dual economy setup, the bulk of the economy was a labour-intensive agricultural sector. Accordingly, this would be a sector that would be producing primary products. Pettinger (2017) further points out that, in his treatise, Arthur Lewis observed that in the agricultural sector described above, productivity would often remain very low. This is due to the fact that farmers would often lack the traditional profit incentive and dynamism usually found in a free economy (Pettinger 2017).

According to Hall (2012), the agricultural sector would be made up of the labourers. These labourers would often be in surplus, and would lack education. Accordingly, the sector itself will be lacking access to capital, which will result in it having reduced chances of economic growth. On this background, the agricultural sector was meant to meet the needs of local markets and only for subsistence.

As indicated earlier that the sector will be characterized by surplus labour, it follows that this sector will ordinarily consists of low wages. Hall (2012) submits that surplus labour results in meagre wage rate that will be near to subsistence level, leading to the marginal productivity of zero. The concept of marginal productivity is defined by Menzies (2018) as "the increase in the total product due to the employment of one more unit of labour". Menzies (2018) further explains that using the concept of marginal productivity, surplus labour in the subsistence sector implies that addition or removal of labour from the subsistence sector does not affect the output of productivity.

On the opposite side of the agricultural sector, which is made up of labourers found in excess and lacking education, and the whole sector lacking access to capital and having reduced chances of economic growth is the industrial sector of the economy. This will be characterized by higher productivity. According to Gollin (2014), the industrial sector is often setup by foreign colonial powers. This sector is further characterized by greater dynamism and an inducement to increase profits through expansion and investment (Gollin 2014).

According to Nipun (2018), Arthur Lewis's argument was that in the face of such disparity in productivity of the two sectors, developing economies could make considerable economic growth by encouraging labour to migrate from the unproductive agricultural sector to the more productive and profitable manufacturing sector (Nipun 2018). This is commonly known as the migration of labour from one sector to the next.

In addition to Nipun's (2018) articulation of Arthur Lewis' argument, Gollin (2014) points out that Arthur Lewis further posited that for overpopulated countries, (which are the focal point of his theory), the central process of development consisted of moving a large mass of underemployed workers with low productivity out of a subsistence sector where living standards are consequently low, into a modern capitalist industrial sector where output per worker is higher due to capital enhancement.

Menzies (2018) point out that Arthur Lewis' model argues for the expansion of the capitalist sector, which requires increased savings, and the attraction of foreign direct investment. The savings and foreign capital, according to Menzies (2018), will be used to generate jobs in the industrial sector. Should there be a shortage of labour in the process, excess labour confined in the agricultural sector will migrate to the industrial sector of the economy.

Assuming that the migrated labour would save its newly found excess income, Pettinger (2017) asserts that the movement of these workers from the low paying jobs in the agricultural sector to the high paying jobs in the industrial sector would raise the savings rate for the economy, thereby consequently igniting a virtuous cycle that gradually increases the level of income per worker in the economy.

In order to understand the tenets of the dual-sector model, Shahzad (2015) and Aditya (2018), highlighted the fact that the dual-sector model contains the following assumptions:

- Population size—Due to the high density of population in less developed countries, many people are disguisedly unemployed, and therefore the marginal productivity of these people is zero.

- The elasticity of labour—accordingly, the supply of labour is perfectly elastic at the subsistence rate of wages.
- The duality of developing economies—accordingly, less developed economies are dual economies, and there is a coexistence of the capitalist sector and subsistence sector.
- The behaviour of owners of capital as economic agents—accordingly, capitalists reinvest all profits.
- Wage differentials between the two sectors of the economy—accordingly, the wage rate is higher in the capitalist sector compared to the subsistence sector.
- Relationship between labour and capital—accordingly, the rate of labour transfer and job creation is proportional to the rate of capital accumulation.

4.3 The Dual-Sector Model and the Key Factors of Production

According to Menzies (2018), Arthur Lewis identified three asymmetries between the industrial sector and the agricultural sector. These are briefly discussed below:

- Technology and factors of production—the industrial sector and the agricultural sector have differences in the technology deployed. However, it was observed that labour was used in both sectors. The production process in the agricultural sector will typically combine labour with land as factors of production. In the industrial sector of the economy, the production process will combine labour with what is referred to as reproducible capital. In explaining the reproducible capital, Vollrath (2009) points out that industrial goods can be consumed or invested, whereas agricultural goods can only be consumed.
- Organization architecture—accordingly, there are organizational differences between the agricultural and the industrial sectors of the economy. On its part, the agricultural sector would be based primarily on subsistence farming. This is contrary to the industrial sector, whose production is based on a modern, market-oriented sector located in urban areas. The commonality between both sectors of the economy is that there is an unlimited supply of labour available.
- The behaviour of owners of capital as economic agents—accordingly, Menzies (2018) points out that Arthur Lewis' third asymmetry has to do with the differences in the behaviour of owners of capital as economic agents in the two sectors. As such, the observation is that the capitalists in the industrial sectors were ambitious. They would save their profits. In the agricultural sector, the landlords would consume most of their income. The lack of liquid capital and growth is probably what explains the lower wage in the agricultural sector.

Looking at the discussion above, we note that Vollrath (2009) makes a deduction from the three asymmetries discussed. Vollrath deduces that it is the profits in the

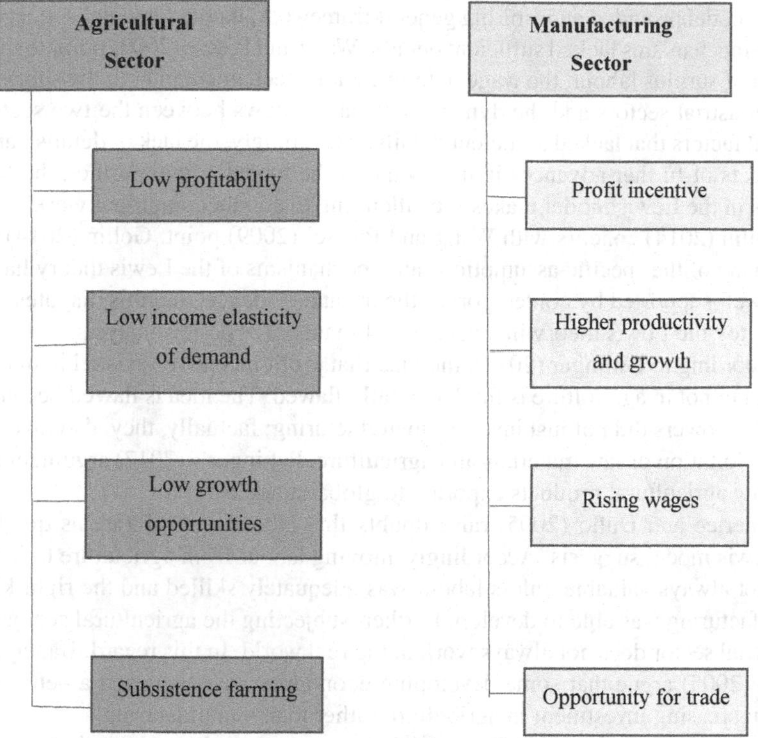

Fig. 4.1 Pettinger's depiction of the dual economy. *Source* Pettinger (2017)

modern capitalist industrial sector that create a growing supply of savings. Accordingly, these profits further finance the formation of an increasing stock of capital, which is later used to employ more and more labour for the industrial workforce. This then fuels growth and further investment opportunities in this sector of the economy. Using the information extracted from Pettinger (2017), the dual economy, as espoused by Arthur Lewis, is depicted in Fig. 4.1.

4.4 Some of the Strengths and Weaknesses of the Lewis' Theory

4.4.1 Weaknesses

Scholars such as Pettinger (2017), Gollin (2014), Wang and Piesse (2009), Banerjee and Newman (1998) and Jorgenson (1961) are among critical voices of the dual-sector economic theory. According to Wang and Piesse (2009), even though the

Lewis model provided an inspiring general framework, its fundamental concepts and micro-mechanisms lacked sufficient details. Wang and Piesse (2009) point to the definition of surplus labour, the wage determination mechanism in both the subsistence and industrial sectors and the dynamics of labour flows between the two sectors as critical factors that lacked sufficient details. Accordingly, the lack of details hampers prospects of further advances in theory along the model's line. Further, the lack of details in the Lewis model makes it challenging to conduct empirical work.

Gollin (2014) concurs with Wang and Piesse' (2009) point. Gollin (2014) states that many of the specific assumptions and mechanisms of the Lewis theory have not been well supported by contemporary theory and evidence, and this disputes efforts to employ the Lewis theory in a very literal manner for policy analysis.

According to Pettinger (2017), the idea that profit incentives existed in manufacturing but not in agriculture is fundamentally flawed. The idea is flawed because the colonial powers did not just invest in manufacturing; factually, they also invested in the exploitation of raw materials and agriculture. Pettinger's (2017) argument is that this saw agricultural products exported to global markets.

Banerjee and Duflo (2005) raise doubts that labour can migrate as quickly as the Lewis model suggests. Accordingly, moving labour from agriculture to industry was not always valuable unless labour was adequately skilled and the right kind of manufacturing was able to develop. Further, subjecting the agricultural sector to the industrial sector does not always work in the real world. In this regard, Banerjee and Duflo (2005) argue that some developing economies have achieved a better return from increasing investment in agriculture rather than manufacturing.

Banerjee and Duflo's (2005) point relating to the interdependence between agriculture and industry has support from Pettinger (2017), who points to a World Bank study that suggested that there was a definite link between growth in industry and growth in agriculture. As such, it was to be expected that if agriculture stagnates it can be challenging to grow the industry.

4.4.2 *Strengths*

According to Ranis (2004), even though the dual-sector model has its limitation, it remains one of the theories that contributed to the field of development economics. Ranis (2004) is of the view that this is one of the fields that is often neglected. Similar to Ranis' (2004) submission, Wang and Piesse (2009) have argued that the advent of the dual-sector theory has had a role in the generation of extensive literature, which today is at the centre of development theory.

A critical contribution of the dual-sector model, which is often not emphasized is its contribution to the concept of transition economies. According to Wang and Piesse (2009), this will be reflected by the transition growth theory, the notion of development phases and sub-phases, en route to modern economic growth. Lewis' model has had a significant role in the development of further theories. In this regard, Kuznet (1955) used it to determine the implications for income distribution, as well as Kuznets' structural analysis of the transitioning economy, as it progresses from agriculture to manufacturing and to services. It can be observed here that this study adopted a dualistic model.

Wang and Piesse (2009) also point out that the Lewis model has not only been used in studying the developing economies. It has also been applied to study labour movements across countries, along with movements among two sectors in the closed economy. Even though the Lewis model has its limitations, Gollin (2014) argues that the Lewis model remains one of the most useful and essential tools for understanding the fundamentals of economic growth. Accordingly, the Lewis model assists in understanding the fundamentals of growth by identifying basic features of the growth process, specifically the importance of within-country gaps in income and productivity or dualism (Gollin 2014).

4.5 Artificial Intelligence and Dual-Sector Model

In reviewing the literature on the dual-sector model, what is clear is that labour is the crucial factor of production in both the agricultural sector and the industrial sector. It is common that in the era that is characterized by technological advances, particularly AI in workplaces, we are beginning to observe considerable parts of the production line taking the automated forms. We think that in areas where it has not, and those areas involve repetitive tasks, the expectation is that this would happen. This affects labour, which is the critical aspect of the dual-sector model.

From the perspective of automated agents, the idea that labour can easily migrate from the sector that is characterized by low levels of education to the industrial sector will falter. Firstly, if we were to suppose the industrial sector is highly capitalized and that profits are reinvested in order to generate efficiencies, the sector will take advantage of machines' efficiencies, and automate. As such, with AI-powered agents such as robots, there may not be employment opportunities in the destiny sector of the economy as Arthur Lewis espoused. Expectations are that factories and the industrial sector will be lean, specialized and consisting of highly skilled human resources that will be working together with machines. Therefore, with leaner factories and the demand for highly skilled resources, there will be no migration.

AI-powered machines are already deployed in the agricultural sector in order to improve yields. The agricultural sector itself, in the era dominated by AI, is not a feeder to the industrial sector but a fully fledged sector that will also be leaner, with machines having a more significant role to play. So, labour could also be expected to experience a squeeze at this front, as the sector moves to become highly capitalized and profits are reinvested in order to generate efficiencies.

4.6 Key Points

- In the dual-sector model, labour is the crucial factor of production in both the agricultural sector and the industrial sector.
- We point out that it is common cause that in the era that is characterized by technological advances, particularly AI in workplaces, we are beginning to observe considerable parts of the production line taking the automated forms. We think that in areas where it has not, the expectation is that this would happen. This affects labour; the critical aspect of the dual-sector model.
- From the perspective of automated agents, we argue that the idea that labour can easily migrate from the sector that is characterized by low levels of education to the industrial sector will falter. Firstly, if we were to suppose the industrial sector as supposed by Lewis that it will be highly capitalized and that profits are reinvested in order to generate efficiencies, the sector will take advantage of machines efficiencies, and automate. As such, with AI-powered agents such as robots, there may not be employment opportunities in the destiny sector of the economy as Arthur Lewis espoused.
- It is our expectation that factories and the industrial sector will be lean as automation intensifies. Our view is that factories will be highly specialized, thus consisting of highly skilled human resources that will be working together with machines. Therefore, with leaner factories and the demand for highly skilled resources, we do not expect any migration of labour from one sector to the next.
- AI-powered machines are already deployed in the agricultural sector in order to improve yields. The agricultural sector itself, in the era dominated by AI, is not a feeder to the industrial sector but a fully fledged sector that will also be leaner, with machines having a more significant role to play. So, we think labour could also expect a squeeze on this front, as the sector moves to become highly capitalized and profits are reinvested in order to generate efficiencies.

References

Aditya H (2018) Lewis model of economic development. www.economicsdiscussion.net/agricultural-economics/lewis-modelof-economic-development/21590. Accessed 17 February 2020

Banerjee A, Duflo E (2005) Growth theory through the lens of development economics. In: Aghion P, Durlauf S (eds) Handbook of economic growth. North Holland, New York

Banerjee AV, Newman AF (1998) Information, the dual economy, and development. Rev Econ Stud 65:631–653

Gollin D (2014) The Lewis model: a 60-year retrospective. J Econ Perspect 28(3):71–88

Hall S (2012) The dual-sector model of economic development: a comparative analysis of Moldova and Romania. Indian J Econ Bus 11(1):107–120

Jorgenson DW (1961) The development of a dual economy. Econ J 71(282):309–334

Kuznet S (1955) Economic growth and income inequality. Am Econ Rev 45(1):1–28

Menzies G (2018) Synthesis of the Lewis development model and neoclassical trade models, no 46. Working paper series from economics discipline group, UTS, Business School, University of Technology, Sydney

Nipun S (2018) The Lewis model of economic development. http://www.economicsdiscussion.net/economic-development/the-lewis-model-of-economic-development/26298. Accessed 17 February 2020

Pettinger T (2017) Dual Economy. https://www.economicshelp.org/blog/10024/developmnent/dual-economy/. Accessed 17 February 2020

Ranis G (2004) Arthur Lewis' contribution to development thinking and policy, Centre discussion paper no 891

Shahzad N (2015) Lewis model and amp; Rastow stages: UAF, education. http://slideshare.net/NaseemCH/lewis-model-amp-rastow-stages. Accessed 17 February 2020

Vollrath D (2009) The dual economy in the Long-Run development. J Econ Growth 4:287–312

Wang X, Piesse J (2009) Economic development and surplus labour: a critical review of the Lewis model. BWPI working paper 89. Brooks World Poverty Institute

Chapter 5
Dynamic Inconsistency Theory

5.1 Introduction

According to Strotz (1955), Laibson (1997) and Augenblick et al. (2015), models of dynamic inconsistency, and time preferences, are pillars of modern behavioural economics. Accordingly, economists have suggested that the dynamic inconsistency theory improved economists' understanding of the tensions involved in consumption, savings choices, task performance, temptation and self-control beyond the general models of exponential discounting.

It would appear that the theory of dynamic inconsistency was initially not associated with economics. Samuelson (1937) and Brocas (2011) have both pointed to Strotz (1955) as the scholar that introduced the theory of dynamic inconsistency into formal economic analysis. The theory made its appearance in his study of optimal intertemporal planning.

The intertemporal planning work sought to showcase the problem of the economic agent selecting a plan of consumption for a later time to maximize current utility. For Samuelson (1937), it is for this reason that the theory of dynamic inconsistency is directly associated with formal economic analysis. Various schools of thought have provided different accounts of what the concept of dynamic inconsistency means. Sections below discuss these various accounts of the concept of dynamic inconsistency.

5.2 Dynamic Inconsistency

According to O'Donoghue and Rabin (1999), dynamic inconsistency could be described as the "circumstances where the optimal plan made by a decision-maker will fail to be optimal as time progresses". Another term that has been used to refer to the concept of dynamic inconsistency is time inconsistency (Strotz 1955).

T. Moloi and T. Marwala, *Artificial Intelligence in Economics and Finance Theories*, Advanced Information and Knowledge Processing,
https://doi.org/10.1007/978-3-030-42962-1_5

What does a dynamic inconsistency attempt to explain? According to Barkan and Busemeyer (2003) and Augenblick et al. (2015), dynamic inconsistency attempts to explain the misalignment of preferences that subsequently lead to inconsistency, which renders the optimal decision in the current time undesirable. According to Strotz (1955), the theory of dynamic inconsistency is usually described as spendthrift. The idea behind this theory being viewed as spendthrift is that it persuades the economic agent to disregard the original optimal plan when acting under budget constraints. Disregarding the original optimal plan occurs if the economic agent has freedom to return to the original optimal plan at a later stage.

Laibson (1997) interprets this as meaning that the economic agent may pre-commit its future economic decision by disregarding any future options so that present desires can be satisfied. It does not end here; according to Strotz (1955), the same economic agent could modify its plans in order to accommodate future deviations. Based on Strotz's (1955) submission, it is not easy to prevent deviation because economic agents are regularly presented with many options with time (Strotz 1955; Augenblick et al. 2015).

According to O'Donoghue and Rabin (1999), because economic agents are consistently presented with many options with time, it follows that the future behaviour of economic agents will be consistent with their optimal plan, based on original expectation. This happens because of the behavioural inconsistency, which is informed by the change in time and circumstances. We depict this discussion using Fig. 5.1.

Suppose, looking at Fig. 5.1, that these balls represent four choices that the economic agent has at a particular time horizon. Suppose that the economic agent is planning for the period that is in the outlook, namely, period T_1. We further suppose that the plan that the economic agent seeks to achieve is consistent with a green ball choices at T_0. Now, this economic agent will pre-commit its future economic decisions to the green ball choices, and other future options, such as red, blue and amber choices will be disregarded so that present desires can be satisfied.

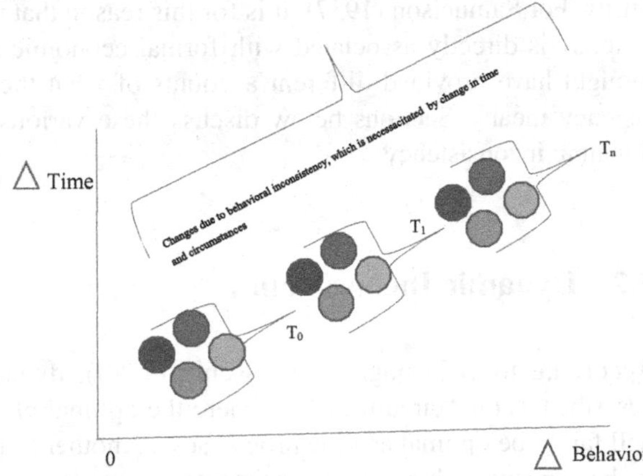

Fig. 5.1 Behavioural inconsistencies necessitated by changes in time and circumstances of an economic agent

As the same economic agent reaches period T_1, they could modify future plans in order to accommodate future deviations. This occurs because time presents economic agents with many options that they may not have considered when making decisions in T_0, given the information at their disposal.

5.3 The Dynamic Inconsistency and the Sure-Thing Principle

In their study, Barkan and Busemeyer (2003) observed that there are three alternative explanations of dynamic inconsistency. We discuss these three alternatives below:

- Firstly, dynamic inconsistency reflects choice inconsistencies alone, which are described as random fluctuations in preferences for similar gamble presented twice. However, Barkan and Busemeyer (2003) go further to prove that, according to choice inconsistency, in terms of gain or losses both outcomes experienced should lead to equal frequencies of risk aversion and risk-seeking inconsistencies. Thus, choice inconsistency alone cannot give a full explanation of the patterns of systematic directions of inconsistency and their dependence on the specific experienced outcome.
- Secondly, in analysing the work of Tversky and Shafir (1992), which itself focused on the analysis of the disjunction effect, Barkan and Busemeyer (2003) and Barkan and Busemeyer (1999) used gambling and observed that when decision-makers imagined either a gain of $200 or a loss of $100 in a first gamble, they were willing to accept a second identical gamble (Barkan and Busemeyer 2003). However, when decision-makers imagined the outcome of the first gamble to be unknown, they rejected the second gamble (Barkan and Busemeyer 1999, 2003). This is referred to as a sure-thing principle. Tversky and Shafir (1992) suggest that the violation of the sure-thing principle came into play as a result of different evaluations of the second gamble. Accordingly, when decision-makers imagine gain or a loss, their evaluations will be made by incorporating the imagined outcome from the first gamble. When decision-makers are faced with an unknown outcome, the evaluation they make will be done without incorporating any information from the first gamble. The different evaluations, as a result, will lead to different utilities, and thus lead to different preferences. Tversky and Shafir's (1992) argument on the dynamic situation at hand suggests that decision-makers incorporate the outcome of the first gamble in the final evaluation of the second gamble, but not in the planned evaluation. Barkan and Busemeyer (2003) go on to assume that instead of considering the second gamble against the possible outcomes of the first gamble, the decision-maker will consider the second gamble against his or her current position. The planned evaluation is made against a current position of zero because he/she has won or lost nothing. The final evaluation is made against a different position corresponding to an actual gain in the first gamble or to an actual loss in the first gamble (Barkan and Busemeyer 2003).

- Thirdly, Barkan and Busemeyer (2003) point out that dynamic inconsistency is based solely on changes in subjective probability rather than in the utility associated with the second gamble. This means that experience will trigger a change in the subjective probability in a manner that will resemble the gambler's fallacy (Barkan and Busemeyer 2003). Accordingly, when planning, the decision-maker will consider the stated probabilities for winning and losing the second gamble (Barkan and Busemeyer 1999). However, experiencing a gain in the first gamble would lead to a decline in the subjective probability associated with another gain in the second gamble. The re-evaluation of the second gamble with a decline in subjective probability for winning will make the same gamble appear less attractive than before, which will lead the decision-maker to obviously reject it. The opposite would happen after the decision-maker experiences a loss; the subjective probability for another loss in the second gamble will decline while the subjective probability for a gain will increase (Barkan and Busemeyer 1999). The re-evaluation of the second gamble would make it seem more attractive than before and could lead the decision-maker to accept it Barkan and Busemeyer (1999, 2003).

5.4 The Time Inconsistency

According to Brocas (2011), the concept of time inconsistency holds that a rational consumer has different dimensions of themselves. This allows these rational consumers to make different decisions in different pockets of time. Accordingly, the existence of imperfect knowledge could be responsible for the difference between the current selves and future selves (Brocas 2011).

According to Brocas (2011), an individual decision-maker could basically be an entity with multiple intra-personal conflicts that span within and between different times. The time effect usually informs the decision variant on behaviour (Barkan and Busemeyer 2003; Brocas 2011). For Barkan and Busemeyer (1999), the inconsistent choices are usually ascribed to an unbridled desire for instant pleasure, a decision clouded by present bias. As such, humans tend to wrongly predict their future marginal utilities by assuming that they will remain at present levels (Barkan and Busemeyer 2003). The assumption that future marginal utilities may remain at present levels leads to inconsistency, as marginal utilities for tastes, desire and gain change over time in a way that the individual did not expect (Brocas 2011).

Hardisty and Pfeffer (2017) posit that the necessity of making consistent decisions between the present and the future gives further credence to the concept of intertemporal uncertainty avoidance in which a decision-maker would prefer the present when the future is uncertain, and would have a preference for the future when the present is uncertain. Hardisty and Pfeffer (2017) found that for both gains and losses, adult decision-makers avoid uncertainty when making intertemporal choices.

Under the rules of political economy, Kydland and Prescott (1977) observe that policymakers have the incentive to deviate from existing contracts made with other agents in the absence of emerging news. Further, forward-looking economic agents, Kydland and Prescott (1977) form expectations about future policy choices, and future policymakers are not likely to remain committed to choices made by the present policymakers.

5.5 What Can We Make of Dynamic Inconsistency in Real Life?

Augenblick et al. (2015) posit that the dynamic inconsistent theory is relevant in the real-life situation at the individual level, group level, firm-level and at the national level. Individuals, firms and governments are consistently faced with making alterations to already set goals in order to accommodate more pressing needs (Augenblick et al. 2015). As such, reducing the effect of time-inconsistency problems could be challenging as that would necessitate more stringent rules (Augenblick et al. 2015). At the individual level, Galperti and Stulovici (2013) contend that to make a forward-looking decision, it requires that the decision-maker discount well being as well as an instantaneous utility to arrive at a realizable future decision at present.

From a socioeconomic perspective, Gibbons (2014) argues that the age of the decision-makers could greatly influence hyperbolic discounting; this relates mostly to emerging adults, who, according to the findings, would behave differently after the age of 30. Millner and Heal (2018) believe that non-dictatorial social preferences could not be stationary. However, where individual decision-makers are discounted utilitarians, there could still be no indication to conclude whether or not individual future preference would be consistent or inconsistent.

In the financial market, for instance, contractual efficiency could be highly impaired by the fact that lenders would abide by the terms of debt contract, whereas the firm could at the same time be facing a dynamically harsh market condition, which threatens violation of covenant restrictions as a result of time difference (Xiang 2019).

Dynamic inconsistency also affects manufacturing companies, and the complication arises from the combination of decisions of customers who would need to purchase complementary products (Gilbert and Jonnalagedda 2011). In such instances, the decision of users, altered by rise in price of other complementary goods produced by different companies, might affect the amount of the other goods purchased and, thereby, the consequential reduction or increase in quantity sold in time and in the future as a result of the external dynamism (Gilbert and Jonnalagedda 2011).

In the field of artificial intelligence, Evans et al. (2016) recognize the relevance of false beliefs and suboptimality that could result from hyperbolic discounting and other biases that often characterize human behaviour. Ordinarily, this could pose a severe challenge in the use of machine learning. However, Evans et al. (2016) demonstrate how such human inconsistency and deviations could be built into algorithms to provide for occasional variation. This is the point of departure from approximate optimality. Dealing with this challenge, the hypothesis of diminishing impatience through time is emphasized by Brocas (2011) as the means of capturing and moderating the behavioural regularity inconsistent with standard exponential discounting (Augenblick et al. 2015).

According to Balaban and Vîntu (2010), monetary policymakers could be exposed to the problem of time inconsistency in pursuance of short-term goals at the detriment of long-term objectives. Possible causes of the inconsistency could be an attempt to bail out strategic intervention during bank distress, miscalculation, competition for limited resources, impatience, immaturity, imperfect knowledge (Balaban and Vîntu 2010; Xiang 2019). Again, it requires that the credibility of commitments to task, policy, plans and decisions must be considered as necessary conditions for ensuring consistency in the future (Bernanke and Mishkin 1997).

This, according to Bernanke and Mishkin (1997), could be moderated by policy as a commitment strategy. Balaban and Vîntu (2010) go on to argue that the time-inconsistency problem can be addressed by giving central banks the primary goal of maintaining the stability of prices and to ensure that the central bank is independent in achieving its targets without government interference. It is their belief that institutional commitment to price stability can enhance the credibility of the monetary policy to improve its performance (Balaban and Vîntu 2010).

Rogoff (1985) also supports the idea of the delegation of monetary policy formulation and implementation to a "conservative" central banker as a way of dealing with the problem of dynamic inconsistency of monetary policy. However, Rogoff (1985) believes that delegation of authority to the central bank does not eliminate the dynamic inconsistency problem, but reduces the inflation bias. In addition, some economists believe that the problem of dynamic inconsistency of monetary policy can be addressed by offering the central banker a performance contract where some of his or her benefits, like salary, are directly linked to the performance of some important macroeconomic variables like gross domestic product and inflation (Walsh 1995; Balaban and Vîntu 2010). Another solution proposed by Balaban and Vîntu (2010) as the most common solution of dynamic inconsistency is the inflation targeting strategy, this because monetary policy authorities are forced to maintain unchanged behaviour as individuals are able to observe at any given time whether the central bank is able to achieve the inflation target or not.

Sadoff et al. (2015) investigated dynamic inconsistency in food choice through a survey experiment of desert food. The natural field experiment was carried out with over 200 customers at a grocery store to investigate dynamic inconsistency and the demand for a commitment to food choice. The study survey discovered substantial dynamic inconsistency, as well as a demand for commitment among a non-negligible number of subjects. The study also established that there were individuals whose demand commitment was more likely to be dynamically consistent in their prior behaviour.

Augenblick et al. (2015) also investigated dynamic inconsistency in terms of working overtime in real effort tasks. The study was building on the failure of many types of research to understand standard patterns of present bias by investigating choices overconsumption, and real effort in a longitudinal experiment. The experiment paired the effort study with a companion monetary discounting study. The results from the experiment confirmed that there was very limited time inconsistency in monetary choices. However, subjects showed considerably more present bias in the effort. Furthermore, the results indicated that present bias in the allocation of work had predictive power for the demand of a meaningfully binding commitment device. The study by Augenblick et al. (2015), therefore, validates a key implication of models of dynamic inconsistency.

Moreover, Maskin and Newbery (1978) extensively explored the problem of dynamic inconsistency. They argued for the case in which large oil-importing countries were choosing the optimum tariff on competitively supplied oil, and the potential existence of dynamic inconsistency for dominant producers has been recognized. The paper by Ulph (1980) is one of the research reports where dynamic inconsistency was recognized. Newbery (1981) argues that dynamic inconsistency arises in the way the maximum principle will find a price path and an associated extraction plan, which, looked at from the present date, maximizes the present discounted profit of the suppliers, on the assumption that the price path will be followed. Newbery (1981) goes on to argue that this is directly equivalent to making an assumption that suppliers will sign binding contracts to follow the extraction plan, where the forecast price path will emerge.

Newbery (1981) also argues that the problem of dynamic inconsistency may also arise at national level in the context of choosing optimal macroeconomic policies for an economy in which agents make their current decisions for issues to do with investment, employment and the like on rational expectations about the future course of the economy as well as the future levels of macroeconomic policies. Maskin and Newbery (1978) submit that the problem of inconsistency of conventionally derived optimal policies is widely recognized in the macroeconomic policy debates, but a satisfactory solution to the problem is still a subject of debate.

Maskin and Newbery (1978) believe that the problem of dynamic inconsistency can also arise for exhaustible resources, and this has been appreciated widely. In contrast to the macroeconomic analysis, a satisfactory solution to the problem of dynamic inconsistency in resources has been found in certain exceptional cases. The models of dynamic inconsistency have many implications in real-life situations on individuals, corporates and governments. For instance, time inconsistency arises when there is an incentive for a decision-maker to deviate from a contract made with another agent even when no news has emerged.

At the individual level, the theory of dynamic inconsistency emphasizes the need for the individual decision-maker to discount personal pleasure in making subsequent choices if future benefits would be attainable. Moreover, at governmental level, when policymakers are applying standing rules, they strengthen and contribute to the attainment of national goals as well as boost government credibility to the public rather than use discretion.

5.6 Artificial Intelligence and the Dynamic Inconsistency Theory

In Fig. 5.1 we supposed that balls represent four choices that the economic agent has at a specific time horizon. Suppose that the economic agent is planning for the period that is in the outlook, namely, period T_1. We further suppose that what the economic agent seeks to achieve is consistent with a green ball choice at T_0. Now, this economic agent will pre-commit its future economic decision to the green ball choices; other future options, such as red, blue and amber choices, will be disregarded so that present desires can be satisfied. As the same economic agent reaches period T_1, they could modify plans in order to accommodate future deviations.

As highlighted earlier, one of the reasons there is a shift from the original pre-commitment is that time present economic agents with many options that they may not have considered when making decisions in T_0, given the information at their disposal. Primarily, we think it is because of the existence of imperfect information. In times where the continued prominence of artificial intelligence and digitization has the emergence of large databases that stores structured and unstructured data, and the presence of AI-powered analytics, our expectation is that the inconsistencies will moderate.

In the previous chapters, we outlined the advantages of intelligent systems as updateability and connectivity (Harari 2018). Using their strength, which lies in these two characteristics, we think intelligent agents will be swift in assisting the economic agent in harvesting information from different sources. Once gathered, this information will be analysed, and it will reduce uncertainties, thus providing the agent with various options. With the ability to store the information, learn about the previous behaviour of the agent and possibly pre-empt the next move that the agent is likely to take, while also providing basket options, AI would awaken the subconscious mind of the agent, in the process challenging the notion of dynamic inconsistency with that of an informed choice.

Economics as a discipline has always provided a well-established foundation for understanding uncertainties and what this implies for decision-making. Agrawal et al. (2018) argue that AI (at least as it is right now) "does not bring us intelligence, but a critical component of intelligence—prediction". In this regard, AI will provide economic agents with a powerful tool that will allow them to make predictions with a certain degree of accuracy.

Using Fig. 5.1, if the economic agent is planning for the period that is in the outlook, namely, period T_1. Moreover, the plan that the economic agent seeks to achieve is consistent with green ball choices at T_0. Now, if this economic agent pre-commits its future economic decision to the green ball choices, other future options, such as red, blue and amber choices would have been disregarded because a plethora of analysed data by AI-powered analytics will be pointing to the fact that they do not satisfy both the present and future desires of that particular economic agent. As the same economic agent reaches period T_1, the expectation is that there should not

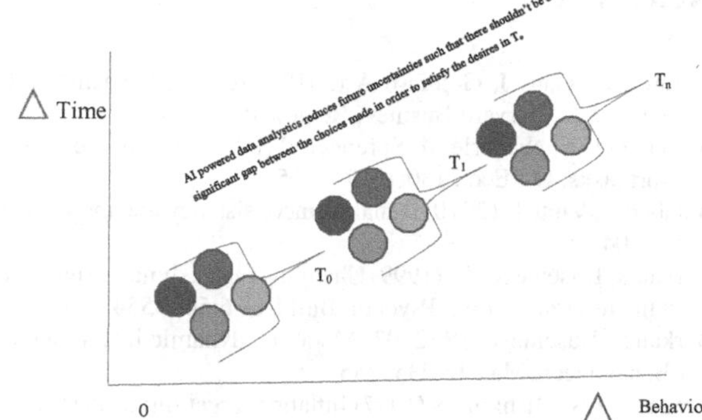

Fig. 5.2 Behavioural inconsistencies necessitated by changes in time and circumstances of an economic agent

be a significant gap between the choices made in order to satisfy the desires in T_o (Fig. 5.2).

5.7 Key Points

- We point out that one of the reasons there is a shift from the original pre-commitment is that time presents economic agents with many options that they may not have considered when making decisions in T_0, given the information at their disposal.
- We think dynamic inconsistency occurs because of the existence of imperfect information.
- In times characterized by prominent utilization of artificial intelligence, and where we realize the emergence of large databases that store structured and unstructured data, our view is that the presence of AI-powered analytics will moderate inconsistencies.
- Using their strength, which lies in the two characteristics above, we think intelligent agents will be swift in assisting the economic agents in harvesting information from different sources. Once gathered, this information will be analysed, and it will reduce uncertainties, thus providing the agent with various options.
- With the ability to store information, learn about the previous behaviour of the economic agent, which are key data sets that allow algorithms to possibly pre-empt the next move that the agent is likely to take, while also providing basket options, we also think that AI would awaken the subconscious mind of the agent, which challenges the notion of dynamic inconsistency with that of an informed choice.
- AI will provide economic agents with a powerful tool that will allow them to make predictions with a certain degree of accuracy.

References

Agrawal A, Gans J, Goldfarb A (2018) Prediction machines: the simple economics of artificial intelligence. Harvard Business Review Press

Augenblick N, Niederle M, Sprenger C (2015) Working over time: dynamic inconsistency in real effort tasks. Q J Econ 130:1067–1115

Balaban G, Vîntu D (2010) Dynamic inconsistency and monetary policy management. MPRA paper no 56042

Barkan R, Busemeyer JR (1999) Changing plans: dynamic inconsistency and the effect of experience on the reference point. Psychon Bull Rev 6:547–554

Barkan R, Busemeyer JR (2003) Modeling dynamic inconsistency with a changing reference point. J Behav Decis Mak 16:235–255

Bernanke BS, Mishkin FS (1997) Inflation targeting: a new framework for monetary policy? J Econ Perspect 11:97–116

Brocas I (2011) Dynamic inconsistency and choice. Theor Decis 71:343–364

Evans O, Stuhlmuller A, Goodman N (2016) Learning the preferences of ignorant, inconsistent agents. In: Thirtieth AAAI conference on artificial intelligence. https://arxiv.org/pdf/1512.05832.pdf

Galperti S, Stulovici B (2013) The logical consistency of time inconsistency: a theory of forward-looking behavior. Discussion papers 1571, Northwestern University, Center for Mathematical Studies in Economics and Management Science

Gibbons BJ (2014) Youth and inexperience: dynamic inconsistency among emerging adults. Ohio University, USA

Gilbert SM, Jonnalagedda S (2011) Durable products, time inconsistency, and lock-in. Manage Sci 57:1655–1670

Harari YN (2018) 21 Lessons for the 21st century. Jonathan Cape, London

Hardisty DJ, Pfeffer J (2017) Intertemporal uncertainty avoidance: When the future is uncertain, people prefer the present, and when the present is uncertain, people prefer the future. Manage Sci 63:519–527

Kydland FE, Prescott EC (1977) Rules rather than discretion: the inconsistency of optimal plans. J Polit Econ 85:473–491

Laibson D (1997) Golden eggs and hyperbolic discounting. Q J Econ 112:443–478

Maskin E, Newbery D (1978) Rational expectations with market power: the paradox of the disadvantageous tariff on oil

Millner A, Heal G (2018) Time consistency and time invariance in collective intertemporal choice. J Econ Theory 176:158–169

Newbery DM (1981) Oil prices, cartels, and the problem of dynamic inconsistency. Econ J 91:617–646

O'Donoghue T, Rabin M (1999) Doing it now or later. Am Econ Rev 89:103–124

Rogoff K (1985) The optimal degree of commitment to an intermediate monetary target. Q J Econ 100:1169–1189

Sadoff S, Samek A, Sprenger C (2015) Dynamic inconsistency in food choice: experimental evidence from a food desert. Becker Friedman Institute for Research in Economics Working Paper

Samuelson PA (1937) A note on measurement of utility. Rev Econ Stud 4:155–161

Strotz RH (1955) Myopia and inconsistency in dynamic utility maximization. Rev Econ Stud 23:165–180

Tversky A, Shafir E (1992) The disjunction effect in choice under uncertainty. Psychol Sci 3:305–310

Ulph AM (1980) World energy models—a survey and critique. Energy Econ 2:46–59

Walsh CE (1995) Optimal contracts for central bankers. Am Econ Rev, 150–167

Xiang H (2019) Time inconsistency and financial covenants. Available at SSRN 3274047

Chapter 6
The Phillips Curve

6.1 Introduction

According to Roberts (1995) and Motyovszki (2013), the concept of the Phillips Curve has been the central theme of macroeconomics from the time it was born in the late 1950s. The core concepts of the Phillips Curve are around the connection of nominal variables such as price and wage inflation and the real economy (Motyovszki 2013). Accordingly, the Phillips Curve seeks to determine how the supply and demand interact in the economy to influence nominal and real variables (Motyovszki 2013; Chugh 2015). Since these variables are central to macroeconomics, Motyovszki (2013) has argued that the Phillips Curve is of crucial importance to policymakers to know more about these relationships.

According to Chugh (2015), an essential feature of the Phillips Curve occurs in the short-run, where there is a depiction of the recurring negative relationship between the inflation rate and the unemployment rate. According to Chugh (2015), despite the fact that there is documented evidence of this much-popularized phenomena, there remains a tense debate in economics about how to model such effect theoretically.

There are several schools of thought in the discipline of economics. Roberts (1995), Motyovszki (2013) and Chugh (2015) have all indicated that one of these schools of thought has totally dismissed the relationship as an unimportant one and, thus, not even worthy of serious theoretical modelling, while the other economists believe that the inflation-unemployment trade-off still drives much policy discussion and is still an essential feature of macroeconomics.

Even with these debates, Roberts (1995), Motyovszki (2013) and Chugh (2015) all point that the Phillips Curve went through a drastic evolution process from its birth. The 1970s was a period characterized by high inflation. As a way of providing solutions to the significant and unexpected economic phenomena such as the high inflation of the 1970s, new schools of thought sprung up with their own versions of the Phillips Curve (Dritsaki and Dritsaki 2013). The different versions brought about policies that ranged from those meant for fine-tuning the real economy to extreme

T. Moloi and T. Marwala, *Artificial Intelligence in Economics and Finance Theories*, Advanced Information and Knowledge Processing,
https://doi.org/10.1007/978-3-030-42962-1_6

ones where demand management policies are ineffective in altering real variables (Dritsaki and Dritsaki 2013; Motyovszki 2013).

In this chapter, we seek to put forward the general basic ideas, history and empirical literature that validate and criticize the Phillips Curve. As indicated in the paragraphs above, there exist different schools of thought in economics. It is inevitable that such diverse schools of thought will find something not necessarily making sense from their point of view.

Even with such criticisms, we argue it is still accepted, that the Phillips Curve offers an invaluable contribution to the measure of the relationship that exists between inflation and the level of unemployment. This could be used as the foundation of policy formulation in an economy. Humphrey (1985:1) is in agreement with this observation, and this is clear where he articulates his position by stating that: "although it may be dismissed as a mere empirical correlation, masquerading as a trade-off, the Phillips Curve relationship between inflation and unemployment has nevertheless been a key component of macroeconomic models for the past 25 years".

6.2 Tenets of the Phillips Curve

Discussions around inflation and unemployment have been the theme of economists' discussions for years (Dritsaki and Dritsaki 2013; Chugh 2015). The economic approach, which looks at unemployment and inflation, appears to have been popularized by the publication of the seminal work by William Phillips in 1958. The seminal work, entitled: "The Relation between Unemployment and the Rate of Change of Money Wage Rates in the United Kingdom, 1861–1957" demonstrated the relationship between unemployment and inflation (Dritsaki and Dritsaki 2013). Phillip's study of the relationship between unemployment and inflation produced an *"inverse relationship between the rate of unemployment and the rate of inflation in an economy"*. In other words, the lower the unemployment in an economy, the higher the rate of inflation (Dritsaki and Dritsaki 2013). This contribution became known as the Phillips Curve and was viewed as a turnaround point in the history of economic theorizing (Hall and Hart 2012; Dritsaki and Dritsaki 2013; Esu and Atan 2017).

Mostly, Phillips found that there was a strong negative relationship between unemployment and inflation, drawing his inferences from UK data (1861–1957). Various scholars have contested these results. A significant body of knowledge has been undertaken to either refute or to validate the conclusions (Esu and Atan 2017). According to Esu and Atan (2017), Paul Samuelson and Robert Solow were the first to test the validity of Phillips' argument, and the results from the tests did support Phillips' argument. The results affirmed the existence of the negative trade-offs between unemployment and inflation in the United States, using pre-1970s and post-1970s data (Esu and Atan 2017). This affirmation by Solow and Gordon was later known as the, *"Solow-Gordon affirmation"* of the Phillips Curve hypothesis (Esu and Atan 2017).

According to Humphrey (1985), since it made its appearance, the Philips Curve has evolved into numerous successive versions. In this regard, the Philips Curve evolved due to the fact that analysts were trying to determine:

- its explanatory power,
- its theoretical content,
- its policy relevance, and
- its ability to fit the facts.

It must be understood that from its inception, the Phillips Curve was an empirical finding (Palley 2012). This evolved, and the theory began to be incorporated into the macroeconomics frameworks. Accordingly, the first theoretical explanation of the Phillips Curve was offered by Lipsey in 1960. Lipsey (1960) argued that the Phillips Curve reflected a process of gradual disequilibrium adjustment in a conventional aggregate labour market (Palley 2012).

Gordon (2008) documents the christening of the curve by Samuelson–Solow in 1975 after it was proposed in 1958 and gained relevance in the field of economics. According to Humphrey (1985), the emergence of the Philips Curve can be traced to the history of inflation that pervaded the world after the world war. The event largely accounted for the motivation behind the crafting of Phillip's Curve, where efforts were made to study the relationship between the rate of inflation and the rate of unemployment within an economy. We depict the Philips Curve in Fig. 6.1.

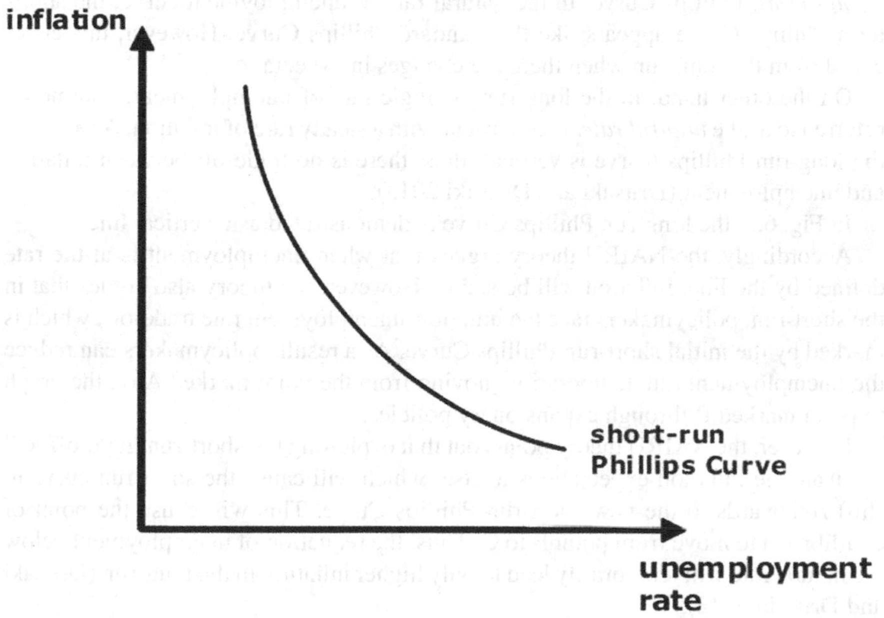

Fig. 6.1 Short-run Phillips curve. *Source* Chugh (2015:149)

Based on Fig. 6.1, Alisa (2015) points out that it is when a fall in unemployment below that natural level is observed that a corresponding rise in wages could occur and vice versa. The curve shows an antithetical relationship between the rate of employment and the rate of increase in wages. This relationship can be explained in a way that demonstrates that an increase in one leads to decrease in the other and vice versa (Humphrey 1985). Alisa (2015) postulates that the inverse could be due to the flexible role of the labour market. Alisa's postulation is based on the premise that several segments within the economy would remain unchanged until there is full employment.

Chugh concludes that based on the proposition of Phillip's Curve, only a combination of some degree of both inflation and the level of unemployment could be possible at a given time if policymakers are to address the two problems in the economy in the short-run (Chugh 2015). The 1970s brought with it the high levels of inflation and unemployment (stagflation). This opened the Phillips Curve to criticism. Those that criticized the Philips Curve pointed out that the relationship that was proposed by the curve was such that the Phillips Curve was a short-run phenomenon (Dritsaki and Dritsaki 2013). According to Dritsaki and Dritsaki (2013), Friedman was one of the critics of the Philips Curve. Friedmans criticism revolved around the fact, in the long-run, there is no trade-off between inflation and unemployment.

As such, a new version of the Philips Curve was proposed. This version is referred to as the *"natural rate of unemployment"*. The natural rate of unemployment curve sought to provide a distinction between the *"short-term"* Phillips Curve and the *"long-term"* Phillips Curve. In the natural rate of unemployment curve, the short-term Phillips Curve appears like the standard Phillips Curve. However, this curve can shift in the long-run when there are changes in expectations.

On the other hand, in the long-run, a single rate of unemployment, commonly referred to as the *natural rate,* is consistent with a steady rate of inflation. As a result, the long-run Phillips Curve is vertical; thus, there is no trade-off between inflation and unemployment (Dritsaki and Dritsaki 2013).

In Fig. 6.2, the long-run Phillips Curve is demonstrated as a vertical line.

Accordingly, the NAIRU theory argues that when unemployment is at the rate defined by the line, inflation will be stable. However, the theory also argues that in the short-run, policymakers face the inflation-unemployment rate trade-off, which is marked by the initial short-run Phillips Curve. As a result, policymakers can reduce the unemployment rate temporarily, moving from the point marked A on the graph to point marked B through expansionary policies.

However, the NAIRU theory points out that exploiting the short-run trade-off will motivate the inflation expectations to rise, which will cause the short-run curve to shift rightwards to the new short-run Phillips Curve. This will cause the point of equilibrium to move from point B to C. Thus, the reduction of unemployment below the natural rate will temporarily lead to only higher inflation in the long-run (Dritsaki and Dritsaki 2013).

Dritsaki and Dritsaki (2013) also argue that when the short-run shift outwards as a result of the need to reduce unemployment, the expansionary policy will result in the worsening of the exploitable trade-off between the unemployment rate and inflation.

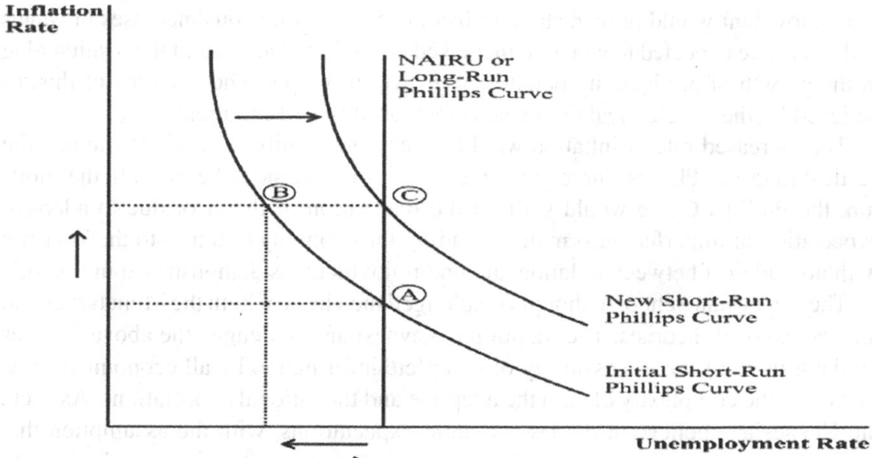

Fig. 6.2 Short-run Phillips Curve and the long-run curve (non-accelerating inflation rate of unemployment—NAIRU) before and after the expansionary policy. *Source* Dritsaki and Dritsaki (2013:4)

The term *"NAIRU"* came as a result of the fact that when the actual unemployment is below NAIRU, inflation accelerates. Contrary to this, when unemployment is above NAIRU, inflation decelerates. Further, when the actual rate of unemployment is equal to NAIRU, the rate of inflation will be stable (Dritsaki and Dritsaki 2013; Alisa 2015).

6.3 Schools of Thought Around the Phillips Curve

As discussed in earlier sections, economics consists of different schools of thought. Like any other theory, the Phillips Curve has received both positive and negative reactions from scholars. Some research has tried to refute it while some have tried to validate its conclusions.

According to Alisa (2015), considering the need to factor in the possible errors of the preceding periods, the Monetarists believe in thc hypothesis of adaptive expectations. The expected inflation rate is conceived as a function of past experience within the economy. On the other side of the spectrum, there is a school of thought that is referred to as the neoclassical school of thought. The neoclassical school believes in the flexibility of price and wages towards producing full employment outputs (Alisa 2015).

Accordingly, it is expected that all the economic agents have full knowledge of the changes in wages and the precise analysis of all the associated economic variables except for the interception of random shocks situation. This view is regarded as a rational expectation. The school believes that changes in aggregate demand would stimulate changes in aggregate supply as well as the level of output, whereas the level of employment would remain static (Alisa 2015). Simultaneous increases in wages and prices are expected to generate increased cost of production and the resultant lag in the growth of productivity behind the growth in wages. The outcome of this, as believed by the neoclassical theorists, is increased rate of inflation.

The increased rate of inflation would necessitate a shift in the short-run and the vertical long-run Philips Curve in the view of the neoclassical theorists. In the short-run, the Phillips Curve would shift on the realization of the error due to adaptive expectation or imperfect information, leading the economy to return to the long-run with no trade-off between inflation and unemployment, as demonstrated in Fig. 6.2.

The Keynesian School of thought challenged the views of both the Monetarists and the neoclassical theorists. The traditional Keynesians challenged the above theories on the ground of the impossibility of complete information by all economic agents as well as the complexity of both the adaptive and the rational expectations. As such, the Keynesians believe in the law of static expectations, with the assumption that an increase in aggregate demand would lead to a corresponding increase in demand for factors of production. Consequently, the effect of static expectations would bring about a decline in unemployment below the natural level, in which case inflation would increase (Alisa 2015).

6.4 Some Criticism of the Phillips Curve

The Phillips Curve hypothesis has been criticized since its inception in the 1960s (Esu and Atan 2017). Islam et al. (2003) also observe that since the inception of the Phillips hypothesis, the theory has gone through intense scrutiny. In the main, Friedman (1968) and Phelps (1968) have been at the forefront of the criticism of the Philips Curve.

The main criticism of the Philips Curve is that the negative relationship between unemployment and inflation is the short-run phenomenon. In the long-run, such a trade-off disappears, a situation where the unemployment rate moves towards the equilibrium, leading to the NAIRU (Friedman 1968; Phelps 1968).

According to Esu and Atan (2017), following the analysis of wage dynamics that took into consideration the union and workers' expectations about future events in the labour market, the Philips Curve suffered some form of decline as a tool for macroeconomic analysis. Friedman (1968), using his natural rate of unemployment hypothesis, convinced many economists on the pointlessness of the monetary policy to attain real objectives in the long-run (Esu and Atan 2017).

According to Lucas (1976), the trade-off between inflation and unemployment could only exist in circumstances where workers are not concerned about the fact that policymakers could create artificial high inflation and low unemployment scenario. However, under normal circumstances, due to fear of future inflation, workers will demand high wages. This scenario will mean that high inflation and unemployment will co-exist, putting the conclusions of the Phillips Curve into disrepute (Lucas 1976; Esu and Atan 2017). This critique, according to Esu and Atan (2017), led to the neglect of the Phillips Curve in the 1980s, though it remains an essential tool for policy formulation (Esu and Atan 2017).

The significant outbreak of the stagflation in the 1970s brought with it a scenario where countries experienced high levels of inflation and high levels of unemployment. The high levels of inflation and high levels of unemployment neutralized the notion of the existence of the negative relationship between inflation and unemployment (Motyovszki 2013; Voinea 2018). Motyovszki (2013) further points out that the existence of stagflation seemed to validate the propositions of Friedman (1968).

For Russell and Banerjee (2008), the 1970s were a period that proved that the assumption of the trade-off between the rate of inflation and unemployed as offered by the Phillips Curve was invalid, especially in the long-run (Russell and Banerjee 2008). Russell and Banerjee (2008) further observed that there was no stable relationship between these two variables during the 1970s. The post-crisis year saw the rates of inflation being subdued, which was another weakness of the Phillips Curve as it could not explain this phenomenon (Voinea 2018).

Esu and Atan (2017) assessed the validity of the Phillips Curve hypothesis in the Sub-Saharan African region. This assessment was done using the panel data technique analysis, and data was drawn from 29 countries in the Sub-Saharan region. In their study, Esu and Atan (2017) used the consumer price index (CPI) as a measure of inflation, while the unemployment rate was measured by total unemployment as a percentage of the total labour force. They found that there was no significant relationship between the inflation rate and the rate of unemployment. The result weakened the existence of the typical Philips Curve relationship, which explains the unemployment–inflation trade-off in the Sub-Saharan African region.

The body of knowledge around the Phillips Curve continues to grow ever since it first made its appearance. Some of this work has found that the relationship does indeed exist between unemployment and inflation. Furthermore, as discussed above, some work weakens the Philips Curve hypothesis. In this regard, Russell and Banerjee (2008) undertook a study that sought to estimate the long-run Phillips Curve, taking into account the non-stationary properties in inflation. They found a small but significant positive relationship between inflation and unemployment. Their results provided evidence to the fact that the trade-off between inflation and unemployment rate in the short-run worsens as the mean rate of inflation increases.

Ogujiuba and Abraham (2013) tested the validity of the Phillips Curve in Nigeria. The study employed the generalized error correction model and the time series data on inflation, unemployment, and gross domestic product from 1970 to 2010. The results showed that the short-run inverse relationship hypothesized between inflation and unemployment by the Philips Curve exists, but it was not significant. In contrast, inflation and unemployment were found to move in the same direction in the long-run.

Further, Dritsaki and Dritsaki (2013) investigated the relationship between inflation and unemployment in Greece using annual data from 1980 to 2010. The study used the cointegration test, and the Granger causality test was obtained by the vector autoregression (VAR). The results of their study showed that there was a long-run and causal relationship between inflation and unemployment in Greece for the period of 1980–2010.

In Romania, Simionescu (2014) tested the stability of the Phillips Curve for from 1990 to 2013. This study concluded that there was a negative relationship between inflation and unemployment rate in the short-run, and that there was a positive relationship in the long-run in the Romanian case. Using the Russian Federation's statistical data, Alisa (2015) investigated the significance of the connection between inflation and unemployment. Upon constructing the short-run and long-run Phillips Curves, Alisa (2015) observed that in general, the Phillips Curve did not apply to the economic situation of Russia in the short-term and the long-term for the years 1999–2015.

Using the distributed lag model with data for the period 1970–2011, Orji et al. (2015) examined the inflation and unemployment nexus in Nigeria by testing the original Phillips Curve proposition for Nigeria. The study discovered a positive relationship between inflation and the unemployment rate in Nigeria.

Govera (2017) investigated the relationship between inflation and unemployment using the South African data for the period 1994–2015. The results confirmed the existence of a positive but insignificant long-run relationship between unemployment and inflation.

Iyeli (2017) also sought to determine whether there exists asymmetry between price expectation and unemployment in the Nigerian economy as indicated by the Philips Curve. The results obtained revealed a direct and positive relationship between inflation and unemployment in Nigeria as against inverse relationship as proposed by the Phillips Curve theory.

Zayed et al. (2018) tested the Phillips Curve by examining the inflation rate, the unemployment rate, annual wage rate, and the gross domestic product of the Philippines for the period of 1950–2017. They found that the results from the Johansen long-run cointegration test showed that there was a long-run relationship among variables, with a positive correlation to inflation during the period 1950–2017. However, the existence of a positive correlation of unemployment rate and the inflation rate was not consistent with the essence of the Phillips Curve. The Phillips Curve predicts an inverse relationship between inflation rate and unemployment rate. The study concluded that the Phillips Curve was not applicable for the economy of the Philippines during 1950–2017.

6.5 Artificial Intelligence and the Phillips Curve

When the Phillips Curve made an appearance into the scene, labour had a considerable role in the production of goods and services. With the countries intensely pursuing technology, we begin to see most factories adopting AI-powered technologies in their production lines. Mostly, we began to see a massive line of production processes being automated.

When a huge part of the production line becomes automated (mechanized), we think the critical aspect of the Philips Curve will be impacted. Both inflation and unemployment variables are key to the Phillips Curve. In the era of artificial intelligence, where a huge part of the production line is expected to be automated (mechanized), we think the key aspect of the Philips Curve will be impacted. Marwala (2007, 2009) have defined artificial intelligence as a technique that is used to make computers intelligent.

In the era where factories are becoming smaller in terms of labour, it is given that the total/partial labour could be out of work because of automation. The expectation is that those that would have been eliminated by the system would be unable to save, pay taxes, or demand goods that will massively be produced by the automated manufacturing factories.

In this automated world, economic growth could be fuelled by robotic infrastructure. Because the robotic infrastructure would have possibly replaced workers, growth would not be accompanied by employment opportunities. At the same time, since this could result in unemployment, the demand for goods and services could be expected to be under pressure. If supply remains the same because the robotic infrastructure will be producing potentially at a higher rate than humans, prices could be expected to decline, dampening inflation prospects.

6.6 Key Points

- The original essential feature of the Phillips Curve is that of the recurring negative relationship between the inflation rate and the unemployment rate.
- Since the Phillips Curve made its appearance, several studies have been conducted to test its hypothesis with varying results. Some of these studies have led to the validation of the Phillips hypothesis, and some have led to its rejection.
- When the Phillips Curve theory was proposed, labour had a considerable role in the production of goods and services. With countries intensely pursuing technology, we begin to see most factories adopting AI-powered technologies in their production lines. Mostly, we are beginning to see a massive line of production processes being automated.
- When a huge part of the production line becomes automated (mechanized), we think the critical aspect of the Philips Curve will be impacted. Both inflation and unemployment variables are key to the Phillips Curve.
- Automation leads to smaller factories. In the era where factories are becoming smaller in terms of labour, it is given that the total/partial labour could be out of work because of automation. Those that would have been eliminated by the system would be unable to save, pay taxes, or demand goods that will massively be produced by the automated manufacturing factories.
- In the automated world, economic growth could be fuelled by robotic infrastructure. Because the robotic infrastructure would have replaced workers, growth would not be accompanied by employment opportunities.
- Since the deployment of smart agents replaces labour, the demand for goods and services could be expected to be put under pressure. If supply remains the same because the robotic infrastructure will be producing potentially at a higher rate than humans, prices could be expected to decline, dampening inflation prospects.

References

Alisa M (2015) The Relationship between inflation and unemployment: a theoretical discussion about the Philips Curve. J Int Bus Econ 3:89–97

Chugh SK (2015) Modern macroeconomics. Massachussets, MIT Press, Boston

Dritsaki C, Dritsaki M (2013) Phillips curve inflation and unemployment: an empirical research for Greece. Int J Comput Econ Econom 3:27–42

Esu G, Atan J (2017). The Philip's curve in Sub-Saharan Africa: evidence from panel data analysis. https://mpra.ub.uni-muenchen.de/82112/

Friedman M (1968) The role of monetary policy. Am Econ Rev 1969(58):102–110

Gordon RJ (2008) The history of the Phillips curve: consensus and bifurcation. Economica 78(309):10–50

Govera H (2017) The relationship between inflation and unemployment. Masters dissertation, University of Western Cape, South Africa

Hall TE, Hart WR (2012) The Samuelson-Solow Phillips curve and the great inflation. Hist Econ Rev 55:62–72

Humphrey TM (1985) The early history of the Phillips curve. Econ Rev, Fed Reserve Bank Richmond, Sep/Oct

Islam F, Hassan K, Mustafa M, Rahman M (2003) The empirics of US Phillips curve: a revisit. Am Bus Rev 21:107

Iyeli EGE (2017) Price expectation and the Philips Curve Hypothesis: The Nigerian Case. Int J Dev Econ Sustain 5(4):1–10

Lipsey RG (1960) The relation between unemployment and the rate of change of money wages rate in the United Kingdom, 1862-1957: a further analysis. Economica 27:1–31

Lucas RE (1976) Econometric policy evaluation: a critique. In: Carnegie-Rochester conference series on public policy, vol 1976, pp 19–46

Marwala T (2009) Computational intelligence for missing data imputation, estimation, and management: knowledge optimization techniques. IGI Global. ISBN: 978-1-60566-336-4

Marwala T (2007) Computational intelligence for modelling complex systems. Research India Publications, Delhi. ISBN: 978-81-904362-1-2

Motyovszki G (2013) The evolution of the Phillips curve concepts and their implications for economic policy. Central European University, Budapest

Ogujiuba K, Abraham TW (2013) Testing the Philips curve hypothesis for Nigeria: are there likely implications for economic growth? Econ Manag Financ Mark 8:59

Orji A, Orji-Anthony I, Okafor J (2015) Inflation and unemployment nexus in Nigeria: another test of the Phillip's curve. Asian Econ Financ Rev 5:766–778

Palley T (2012) The economics of the Phillips curve: Formation of inflation expectations versus incorporation of inflation expectations. Struct. Chang Econ Dyn 23:221–230

Phelps ES (1968) Money-wage dynamics and labor-market equilibrium. J Polit Econ 76:678–711

Phillips AW (1958) The relation between unemployment and the rate of change of money wage rates in the United Kingdom, 1861–1957. Economica New Ser 25(100):283–299

Roberts JM (1995) New Keynesian economics and the Phillips curve. J Money Credit Bank 27:975–984

Russell B, Banerjee A (2008) The long-run Phillips curve and non-stationary inflation. J Macro Econ 30:1792–1815

Simionescu M (2014) Testing the existence and stability of Phillips curve in Romania. Monten J Econ 10:67

Voinea L (2018) Explaining the post-crisis Philips curve: cumulated wage gap matters for inflation. CEPS Working Document No 2018/05, June 2018

Zayed NM, Islam MR, Hasan, KR (2018) Testing Phillips curve to examine the inflation rate regarding unemployment rate, annual wage rate and GDP of Philippines: 1950–2017. Acad Account Financ Stud J

Chapter 7
The Laffer Curve

7.1 Introduction

According to Mirowski (1982), the Laffer Curve was first made public in different newspapers, but it also made its appearance in the book published by Jude Wanniski in 1978. Historical records indicate that there had been antecedents of this on the writings from the Middle East and that of JM Keynes. The term Laffer Curve was popularized by the Wall Street Journal reporter (Mirowski 1982). Accordingly, Arthur Laffer argued, in the Laffer Curve, that at a certain point, there exists no positive correlation between government tax rates and revenues. In fact, after a specific tax rate threshold, the relationship turns to become negative. Accordingly, this was contrary to the popular opinion of the time, which had been advanced by economists such as John Maynard Keynes. The idea that at a particular tax threshold point, there exists no positive correlation between tax rates and revenues, therefore, contradicted the long-held principle around the relationship between tax rates and government revenues.

In his notes, Arthur Laffer advanced an argument that changes in tax rates affect government revenues differently in the short term and the long basis. On the short-term basis, Altunoz (2017) describes it as the "arithmetic effect in which every dollar in tax cuts translates directly to one less dollar in government revenue". On the other hand, the longer term effect is described as the "economic" effect during which Laffer believes lower tax rates imposed by the government bring about an increase in the amount of money available for investment purposes in the hands of the taxpayers (Altunoz 2017).

In Arthur Laffer's view, the long-term effect creates more business activity to meet consumer demand at the individual level. At the corporate level, firms would be able to afford to hire more workers, increase productivity and generate a broader tax base, which would invariably stimulate economic growth. Based on this premise, Laffer contended that government revenue, which appeared lost at the tax cut, could then be recovered.

T. Moloi and T. Marwala, *Artificial Intelligence in Economics and Finance Theories*, Advanced Information and Knowledge Processing,
https://doi.org/10.1007/978-3-030-42962-1_7

In this chapter, we examine the tenets of the Laffer curve, which defines the relationship between tax revenue and the tax rate. We study the impact of the advances in automation and its impact on tax collection. In particular, we study how advances in AI are changing the very nature of the Laffer curve. We discuss the tenets of the Laffer Curve, followed by the criticism of the curve and, finally, the implication of artificial intelligence on the Laffer Curve.

7.2 Tenets of the Laffer Curve

According to Laffer (2009), the principle upon which the Laffer Curve operates is rooted in the analysis and understanding of individual behavioural responses to taxation. This is said to be the potential explanatory of the shape of the Laffer Curve. Accordingly, the process of how individuals arrive at decisions regarding consumption and leisure is germane to the operation and application of the Laffer curve. The theoretical basis for these explanations is that individuals change their behaviour when a tax rate is raised or lowered, and the government rate of tax is believed to distort the optimal choices of an individual when after-tax prices change (Laffer 2009).

In Arthur Laffer's view, if the government was to raise the personal income tax rate, for instance, the likelihood is that individuals could select to work lesser and, thus, to spend more of their time on leisure. This view would be problematic in the global context. For instance, developing countries often face an army of people that are seeking employment. The fact that some developing countries would not necessarily have the social security system that is found in developed countries simply tells us that the choice of dropping a job for more leisure because of movements in the personal income tax rate would not hold.

Looking at the capital gains tax, Laffer (2009) points out that the individual's choice to delay or hasten capital gain tax payment could also influence their decision to substitute present consumption for the future and vice versa depending on where the tax rates are moving. Capital gains are "a levy assessed on the positive difference between the sale price of the asset and its original purchase price" (Investopedia 2019).

Figure 7.1 illustrates the Laffer Curve. The Laffer Curve demonstrates that at specific tax rates, in this regard the 60% tax rate, tax revenues will begin to decline. Essentially, what this means is that there will be no incentives for increasing a tax rate beyond a certain point.

As can be seen in Fig. 7.1, as tax rates increase from zero taxes level upward, the amount of revenue generated from taxes also increases, pointing to a positive relationship at this point. The flatness of the curve shows the pattern of taxpayers' responses to the level of increment in the rate of taxes. At the point where the taxpayers can no longer bear the excessive burden of the taxes, their unwillingness is depicted by the steep in the curve, at which point, much revenue is lost to the increased rate. At this point, there is a negative relationship between tax rates and government revenue.

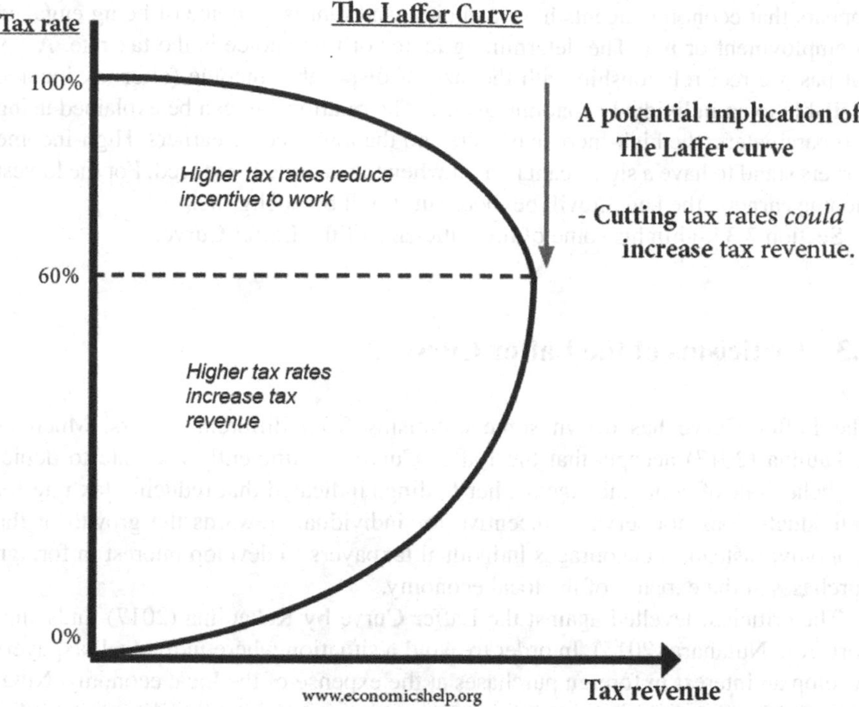

Fig. 7.1 The Laffer curve (*Source* Pettinger (2019) from Economicshelp.com 2019)

Hsing (1996) has argued that at the national level, increased tax rate poses a burden on economic growth as this forces demand to fall in a more extended period, which diminishes the tax base as shown by the backward movement of the curve. Laffer (2009) describes the point from where the curve tends backward as "Prohibitive Range".

Beyond the prohibitive point, additional taxes result in reduced government revenue. If this continues, the curve shows that government revenue would decline until the point of zero, where no revenue would be generated by the government (Hsing 1996). The resultant effect of the continuous increase in tax rate is general disincentives for people to work harder and to invest (Karas 2012).

The point made above by Karas (2012) is in line with the observation that there exists some form of relationship between tax and the investment behaviour of economic agents. Therefore, the relationship is that economic agents will monitor the tax cycles. In cycles where taxes are higher, it appears that the Laffer Curve would see economic agents withdrawing their services because there is little incentive to continue working. In a higher tax rate environment, the Laffer Curve suggests that there will be reduced disposable income, reduced savings and reduced investments.

Similarly, if tax rates were to be reduced, the Laffer Curve suggests that this will lead to higher disposable income, higher savings and higher investments. Here, it appears that economic agents have a choice, and that is a choice of being engaged in employment or not. The determining factor of this choice is the tax rate. A tax cut has a direct relationship with the size of disposable income (after-tax income available to an individual economic agent). The relationship can be explained using two parameters, the high-income earners and the low-income earners. High-income earners stand to have a significant benefit when the tax rate is reduced. For the lowest income earners, the benefit will be there but it will be negligible.

Section 7.3 highlights some of the criticisms of the Laffer Curve.

7.3 Criticisms of the Laffer Curve

The Laffer Curve has drawn some criticisms from different sectors. Much as Kakaulina (2017) accepts that the Laffer Curve is sufficiently accurate to depict the behaviour of economic agents, her findings indicated that reducing tax rate for individuals does not serve as incentive for individuals towards the growth of the economy; instead, it encourages individual taxpayers to develop interest in foreign purchases at the expense of the local economy.

The criticism levelled against the Laffer Curve by Kakaulina (2017) finds support from Nutahara (2015). In order to avoid a situation where individual taxpayers develop an interest in foreign purchases at the expense of the local economy, Nutahara (2015) offers solutions by using Japan as a case. In this regard, he suggests that the government should increase the rate of labour tax (Pay as You Earn) and decrease the capital tax rate. Accordingly, this could increase tax revenues.

According to Mirowski (1982), some things went wrong with the Laffer Curve. These things include the magnitude of elasticities of incentives, the problems of empiricism, the omission of other potentially relevant variables and, lastly, the subsidiary controversy about the size of the underground economy (Goolsbee 1999). We further expand on the things that Mirowski thinks went wrong with the Laffer Curve as follows:

- **The magnitude of elasticities of incentives**: Mirowski (1982) critiqued the fundamental argument of Laffer concerning the claim that taxation might turn to incentives. The counter-argument against such claim hailed from the fact that the number of hours worked by taxpayers in the primary labour markets are not dependent on their discretion but on institutional rules and considerations. As such, the conventional eight-hour per day could not be altered by workers in a bid to show they are wary of the tax burden.
- **Problems of empiricism**: Mirowski (1982) and Goolsbee (1999) point out that the concept of the Laffer curve hinges on the relationship between a tax cut and government revenue. Now, this relationship was established, Mirowski (1982) and Goolsbee (1999) argue based on the historical events of the Mellon-Harding 1921 tax cut, the 1964 Kennedy Tax cut and the 1978 Romero Barcelo tax cut, which were followed by accelerated economic growth.

- **The omission of other potentially relevant variables**: Mirowski (1982) argues that the fundamental flaw of the Laffer Curve is that it is a single-variable model. Mirowski (1982) points out that there is no single tax rate for any actor, whether as an individual, a firm or an economy. According to Mirowski (1982), other variables could have formed part of the Laffer Curve but were excluded, hence the criticism of the single-variable model. The Laffer Curve excludes essential variables such as levels of investment and consumption, interest rate, corporate leverage and the balance of trade.

The advent of new technologies has resulted in a change in the manner in which things are done. Improvement in technology and its adoption has led to many changes. In Sect. 7.4 below, we discuss how theories such as the Laffer Curve can be approached and understood in the context of artificial intelligence.

7.4 Artificial Intelligence and the Reconsideration of the Laffer Curve

According to Li (2013), Artificial Intelligence (AI) is "a new science and technology which studies theories, mechanisms, developments and applications on how to simulate human intelligence via computerized robots, voice recognition, image recognition, natural language processes and expert systems". This definition is consistent with that of Feldman (2001), where "AI is seen as about giving machines the capability of mimicking human behaviour, mainly cognitive functions". Examples would be facial recognition, automated driving and sorting mail based on postal code. Finally, Marwala (2018) defines artificial intelligence as a computational technique for intelligent building machines, which has in the past been used successfully to model complex problems.

In all these definitions, what is clear is that machines will simulate or mimic human intelligence. In the context of these definitions, the Laffer Curve is designed around labuor as a factor of production. In the tenets of this theory, the government will generate income from taxation. At a certain point (if the tax rate continues to increase), the income generated will not be in tandem with the tax rate.

If we were to consider one company that decides to automate its production line, that particular company would not necessarily need to collect the Pay As You Earn (PAYE), which is the personal income tax, on behalf of the government. This is because the robotic infrastructure with artificial intelligence will be performing tasks that are performed by human beings, and not being paid salaries. We made the point in the previous chapter that machines do not get tired, bored or ask for leave of absence. In this hypothetical company, no matter how many movements are in the tax rate, until the government introduces taxes, say on computerized robots, it will not derive any revenue, and then the theory will not hold.

In the case of corporate tax, we are of the view that the introduction of AI does not affect the theory. We are further of the view that the theory will still hold. Initially, the increase in the corporate tax rate will be followed by an increase in tax revenues generated by the government. This will continue until it reaches the prohibitive point. Once more, beyond the prohibitive point, additional taxes result in reduced government revenue. If this continues, the curve shows that government revenue would decline until the point of zero where no revenue would be generated by the government (Fig. 7.2).

Figure 7.3 represents our thinking around the tax movement that is likely going to happen. We think that with machines having replaced human beings (full or part automation), government revenue will be represented by the red line in Fig. 7.3, indicating that it will be lower than the case before the introduction of intelligent machines. Our view is that there is an opportunity for the government to increase

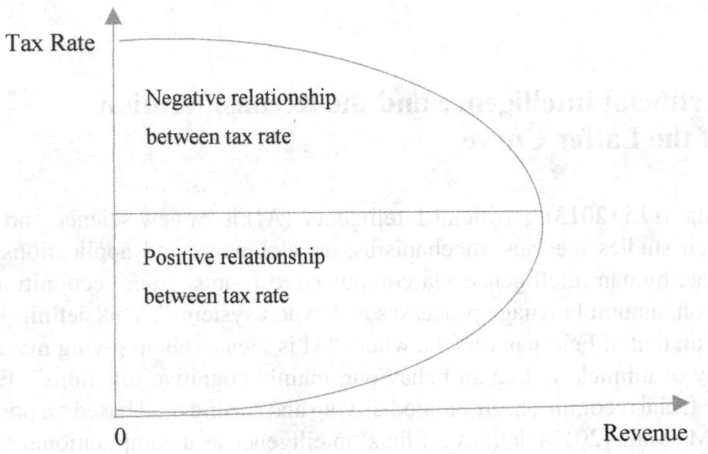

Fig. 7.2 The effect of AI on the Laffer curve (corporate tax) (*Source* Authors' compilation)

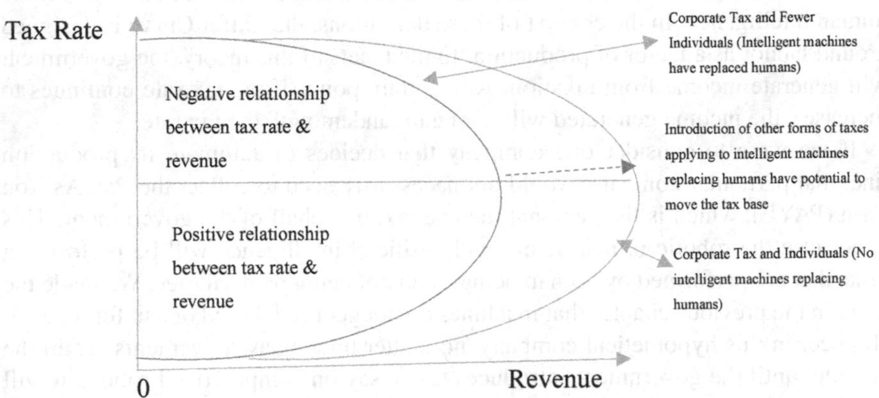

Fig. 7.3 The effect of AI on the Laffer curve (personal income tax, corporate tax and other related taxes)

Fig. 7.4 Multivariable AI based model

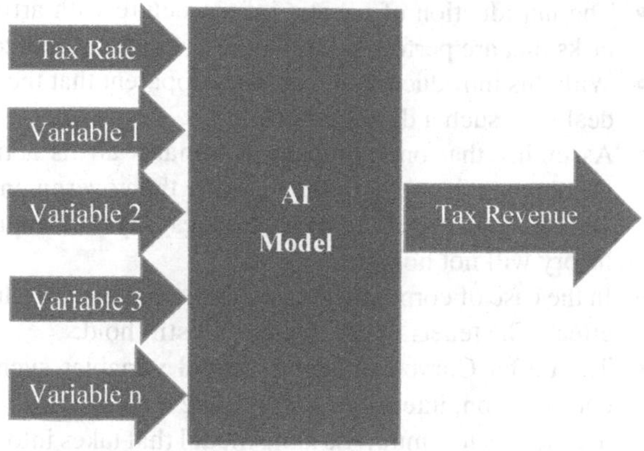

Where N represents the population

tax revenues, which is by introducing some form of taxes on robots. The grey arrow in Fig. 7.3 represents that movement, which would push revenues up. However, it should be noted that the principle around the prohibitive point still holds.

In earlier sections, we pointed out that Mirowski (1982) argues that the fundamental flaw of the Laffer Curve is that it is a single-variable model. Mirowski (1982) further points out that there is no single tax rate for any actor, either as an individual, a firm or in an economy. According to Mirowski (1982), other variables could have formed part of the Laffer Curve but were excluded, hence the criticism of the single-variable model. Accordingly, the Laffer Curve excludes essential variables such as levels of investment and consumption, interest rate, corporate leverage and the balance of trade. AI can be used to create a multi-variable model that takes into account variables suggested by Mirowski.

The model could take the form of Fig. 7.4.

7.5 Key Points

- Arthur Laffer argued, in the Laffer Curve, that there existed no positive correlation between government tax rates and revenues. This was contrary to the popular opinion of the time, which had been advanced by economists such as John Maynard Keynes.
- According to the theory, initially, the increase in the corporate tax rate will be followed by an increase in the tax revenue generated by the government. This will continue until it reaches the prohibitive point.
- Beyond the prohibitive point, additional taxes result in reduced government revenue.
- If this continues, the curve shows that government revenue would decline until the point of zero, where the government would generate no revenue.

- The introduction of robotic infrastructure with artificial intelligence to perform tasks that are performed by human beings neutralizes the Laffer Curve.
- With this introduction, it becomes apparent that the Laffer Curve was not built to deal with such a development.
- Assuming that one company automates all its activities, no matter how many movements there are in the tax rate, the government will not derive any revenue until the government introduces taxes, say on computerized robots. This way, the theory will not hold.
- In the case of corporate tax, we think that the introduction of AI does not have an effect. The tenets of the theory will still hold.
- The Laffer Curve excludes essential variables such as levels of investment and consumption, interest rate, corporate leverage and the balance of trade. AI can be used to create a multi-variable model that takes into account these variables as we suggest in Fig. 7.4.

References

Altunoz U (2017) The application of the laffer curve in the economy of turkey. J Int Soc Res 10:654–659

Feldman, J. (2001). Artificial intelligence in cognitive science. Int Encycl Soc Behav Sci 792–796. https://doi.org/10.1016/B0-08-043076-7/01613-2

Goolsbee A (1999) Evidence on the high-income Laffer curve form six decades of tax reform. Brookings Papers on Economic Activity, 2. https://www.brookings.edu/wp-content/uploads/1999/06/1999b_bpea_goolsbee.pdf

Hsing Y (1996) Estimating the Laffer curve and policy implications. J Soci Econ 25(3):395–401

Investopedia (2019) Capital gains tax. https://www.investopedia.com/terms/c/capital_gains_tax.asp. Accessed 3 Sept 2019

Kakaulina MO (2017) Visual representation of Laffer curve factoring in implications of capital outflow. J Tax Ref 3(2):103–114

Karas M (2012) Tax rate to maximize the revenue: Laffer curve for the Czech Republic. J Soc Econ 60(4):189–194

Laffer AB (2009) The Laffer curve: thinking economically. Texas Policy Foundation. https://files.texaspolicy.com/uploads/2018/08/16093009/When-You-re-Right.pdf

Li L (2013) The future of academic libraries in the digital age, trends, discovery, and people in the digital age 253–268. https://doi.org/10.1016/B978-1-84334-723-1.50016-4

Marwala T (2018) Handbook of machine learning: foundation of artificial intelligence, Vol 1. World Scientific Publication. ISBN: 978-981-3271-22-7

Mirowski P (1982) What's wrong with the Laffer curve? J Econ Issues xvi(3):815–828

Nutahara K (2015) Laffer curves in Japan. J Jpn Int Econ 36:56–72. https://doi.org/10.1016/j.jjie.2015.02.002

Pettinger T (2019) The Laffer curve. Available from https://www.economicshelp.org/blog/140859/economics/the-laffer-curve/

Chapter 8
Adverse Selection

8.1 Introduction

This chapter discusses the theory of adverse selection in the context of artificial intelligence. Economics, risk management and insurance are disciplines that employ both the concepts of moral hazard and adverse selection (Akerlof 1970). Adverse selection occurs when one agent in a transaction has more information than the other party, thus giving it an advantage. Primarily, the partner with more information would use it to strategically position itself (strategic behaviour) against the interest of the less informed counterparty in a transaction (Belli 2001).

It is evident in Akerhof (1970) and Belli (2001) that, essentially, adverse selection is a problem that stems from information asymmetry, where a strategic behaviour by the more informed counterparty in a contract works against the interest of the less informed counterparties (Almeida 2014; Belli 2001). Since most information in a market-driven economy is transmitted through pricing, adverse selection will result in unfair pricing of goods and services and unfair advantage on the part of the counterparty with more information. The modern world, however, is highly characterized by digitization, which ensures access to more information about the counterparty in the transaction.

This chapter examines how the adverse selection theory will look like in a situation where the information is produced and stored by the intelligent systems, and a scenario where the information is digitally available and easily accessible by all parties in the transaction.

The fourth industrial revolution is an era characterized by artificial intelligence and other technologies. Marwala (2018) views artificial intelligence as "a computational technique for building machines that are intelligent". In the past, this technology has been used successfully to model complex problems such as HIV (Marwala 2007).

Further, artificial intelligence has been deployed to make decisions with missing information (Marwala 2009; Leke and Marwala 2019), to model mechanical machines (Marwala 2010; Marwala et al. 2017), to understand interstate conflict

T. Moloi and T. Marwala, *Artificial Intelligence in Economics and Finance Theories*, Advanced Information and Knowledge Processing,
https://doi.org/10.1007/978-3-030-42962-1_8

(Marwala and Lagazio 2011), for detection of faults in mechanical and electrical structures (Marwala 2013), to model economic and financial systems (Marwala 2013; Marwala and Hurwitz 2017), in croud sourcing (Xing and Marwala 2018a), in robotics (Xing and Marwala 2018b) and to model causality (Marwala 2014, 2015).

8.2 Adverse Selection

Akerlof (1970) was the first scholar and contributor to what the effect of information asymmetry is. In the paper titled *The Market for Lemons*, he sought to explain why the market for used cars—some of which may be mechanically deficient *lemons*—does not function well (Akerlof 1970). To explain Akerlof's (1970) logic, Gezina (just outside Tshwane, formerly known as Pretoria, the administrative capital of South Africa) is full of second-hand motor vehicle dealerships. Supposedly, one of these dealerships has two similar-looking cars. The difference between these two cars is how the previous owners would have handled them. In our supposition, one of the cars would have been well handled. It would have been appropriately taken care of, i.e. the car would have been serviced at the right intervals.

The second car, however, has not been well looked after. In this regard, the previous owner would not have maintained (duly serviced) the car at the right intervals. It could be that several services were missed. Further, it has had damage to the rear bumper, which was later fixed (effectively it is an accident damaged vehicle).

In selling the car to the dealerships, the previous owner of "the damaged" vehicle did not disclose its previous condition. We suppose that the dealership secured these two motor vehicles for R100 000 each (~$7142 each). Had the dealership known that one of the vehicles is an accident damaged vehicle, it would not have paid R100 000. It would have paid far much less than what it paid. The lack of information in the accident damaged and insufficiently serviced car has undermined the decision-making of this dealership. Akerlof (1970) refers to this as market failure and a classic case of adverse selection.

Following the publication of Akerlof's (1970) seminal work on information asymmetries, a wide range of literature was devoted to understanding the consequences of information asymmetries. Following this seminal work, studies around information have become so important that there is a body of work that focuses on information asymmetries in economic and management sciences.

Several other scholars such as Wilson (1993), Laffont and Tirole (1993), Freixas and Rochet (1997) and Diamond (1998) have all demonstrated how information asymmetries play a fundamental role in the adverse selection which is consistent with our example of a dealership in Gezina. In other words, these scholars seek to demonstrate the consequences of information asymmetries in economic decisions making by economic agents. In this regard, and using our example of the dealership in Gezina, it becomes apparent that all rational economic and financial decisions should be based on a certain degree of information.

As such, Akerlof (1970) demonstrates that information is the basis for any economic and financial decisions taken by economic agents, whether they are consumers or corporates. For economic agents, whether consumers or corporates, to be in a position to make sound judgments, there is a need for information before the transaction is entered into. Our example of the dealership in Gezina demonstrates that the market will perform poorly or fail to perform should there be a lack of complete information.

8.3 Adverse Selection and the Agency Problem

Moloi (2009) notes that in *The Theory of the Firm*, Jensen and Meckling (1976) examined the relationship between principals and agents in a company. This seminal work proposed the theory of the firm, based upon conflicts of interest between various contracting parties, namely, shareholders, managers and debt-holders (Moloi 2009).

Eisenhardt (1989), cited by Moloi (2009), observes that the agency theory refers to the ever-present agency relationship in companies, where one party (the principal) delegates work to another (the agent), who has to perform that work, i.e. the principal mandates the agent to do a certain task and the agent is remunerated for that task. Figure 8.1 demonstrates the agency relationship, and how it is typically managed.

Moloi (2009) observes that Eisenhardt (1989) argued that under conditions of imperfect information and uncertainty, which is the situation in most companies, because of the complex shareholding, for example, in public companies, two agency problems arise. These problems are known as adverse selection and moral hazard.

The first problem arises when the desires or goals of the principal and those of an agent conflict. Since the principal is detached from the day-to-day operations of

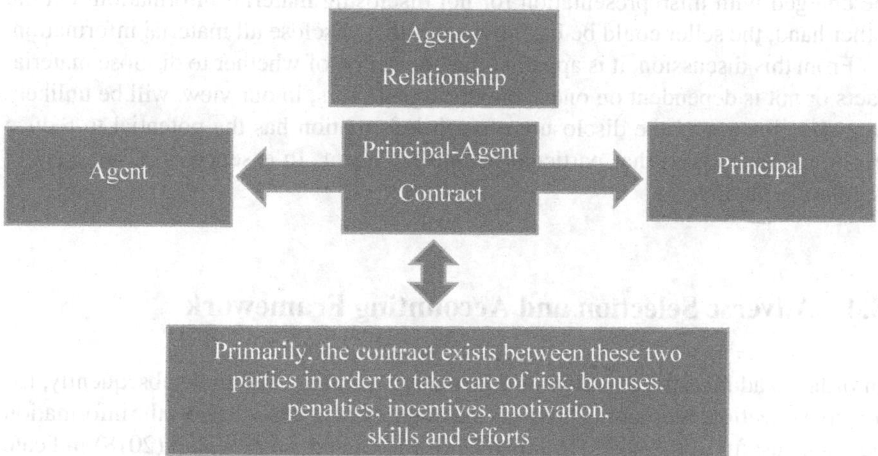

Fig. 8.1 The agency relationship, and how it is typically managed (*Source* Moloi (2009)—information was sourced from Tiessen and Waterhouse (1983: 251–267))

the business, and the decisions that are made by the agent, the principal may not be certain that decisions taken by the agent are in the interest of the corporation.

The principal will seek the assistance of other parties (auditors, appointing the board) to moderate the behaviour of the agent. This is because it is difficult to monitor the behaviour of the agent if the principal is not there on a day-to-day basis. The cost of verification is borne by the principal. This is sometimes referred to as the agency cost. The principal embarks in this process simply because the principal cannot verify that the agent has behaved appropriately. Eisenhardt (1989) refers to this situation as an adverse selection.

The second agency problem arises when both the principal and agent have different attitudes towards risk. The problem here is that the principal and the agent may prefer different actions because of their different risk preferences. This is known as a moral hazard (Eisenhardt 1989).

Several researchers, such as Stiglitz and Weiss (1981), have also observed both the moral hazard and the adverse selection challenges, albeit in the context of credit rationing theory of banks. In this regard, citing Stiglitz and Weiss (1981), Moloi (2009) asserts that the core of the Stiglitz and Weiss model is the theory of asymmetric information. Information is said to be asymmetric if it is not freely available. This causes the information to be unevenly distributed among the agents, which is consistent with Akerlof (1970), Wilson (1993), Laffont and Tirole (1993), Freixas and Rochet (1997) and Diamond (1998). AI and the agency theory are discussed in Chap. 11 of this book.

To address the agency problem, which subsequently results in adverse selection due to the asymmetric information between economic agents, scholars such as Tiessen and Waterhouse (1983) have suggested that there should be penalties or incentives so that transparent behaviour is promoted. In our example of a dealership in Gezina, what this means is that the seller of an accident damaged motor vehicle could be charged with misrepresentation for not disclosing material information. On the other hand, the seller could be incentivized if they disclose all material information.

From this discussion, it is apparent that the action of whether to disclose material facts or not is dependent on one economic agent. This, in our view, will be unlikely in a situation where the disclosure of such information has the potential to reduce economic benefits to that particular economic agent. In essence, it is not easy to regulate behaviour.

8.4 Adverse Selection and Accounting Framework

In order to address the question of information asymmetries and, subsequently, the adverse selection, accounting literature has attempted to describe how the information becomes useful to the users. In this regard, Moloi and Adelowotan (2018) indicate that the international financial reporting standard (IFRS) framework describes the basic concepts that underlie the preparation and presentation of financial statements for external users (International Accounting Standards Conceptual Framework (IAS) 2010).

In order to address the question of information asymmetries and subsequently the adverse selection, IAS (2010) gives guidance that the information (financial information in the context of the IAS) is useful when it is relevant and represents what it purports to represent accurately. It is essential that both relevance and fair presentation are seen as the fundamental qualitative characteristics.

In order to address the challenge similar to what Akerlof (1970) raised, the IAS Conceptual Framework (2010) would respond by stating that the disclosure and making available relevant information (financial information in the context of the IAS) can make a difference in the decision-making process. The IAS is convinced that once the information is relevant and fairly presented, it could then be useful to the decision-making process. Further, the IAS (2010) is of the view that the usefulness of financial information is enhanced if it is comparable, verifiable, timely and understandable. These four factors are described below:

- Comparability—the information about the organization under review can be useful if "it can be compared with similar information about other entities and with similar information about the same entity for another period or another date. As such, comparability enables users to identify and understand similarities in, and differences among, items" (IAS Conceptual Framework 2010).
- Verifiability—the information about the organization under review can be useful if it is verifiable. As such, this concept assists in assuring users that information faithfully represents the economic phenomena it purports to represent. Verifiability is a situation where "different knowledgeable and independent observers could reach consensus, although not necessarily complete agreement, that a particular depiction is a faithful representation" (IAS Conceptual Framework 2010).
- Timeliness—the information about the organization under review is said to be timely if it can be made available "to decision-makers in time to be capable of influencing their decisions" (IAS Conceptual Framework 2010).
- Understandability—the information about the organization under review is said to be understandable if it can be classified, characterized and presented clearly and concisely. The IAS Conceptual Framework (2010) concedes that some phenomena within the reports could inherently be complex, rendering them not easily understood; however, excluding them solely on the basis that they are complex will make these reports "incomplete and potentially misleading" (IAS Conceptual Framework 2010).

The main difficulty with the IAS (2010) framework is that economic agents in the transaction have a divergent interest. One party in a transaction would always have a piece of better information than the other. In the case of our dealership in Gezina, the owner of the accident damaged car has a piece of better knowledge about the problems of the motor vehicle than the dealership to which the motor vehicle was subsequently sold.

What the IAS is asking is that the economic agent should work against maximizing what he/she could potentially receive as the proceeds of the sale of the motor vehicle to the dealership if this information were to be kept by him/her. The IAS (2010) appears to be appealing to the conscience or ethics that economic agents should do what is morally correct. This is clear from the use of the word "fair".

8.5 Artificial Intelligence and Its Impact on Adverse Selection

In their work, *The Identification and Estimation of Incentive Problems: Adverse Selection*, d'Haultfoeuille and Février (2007) lament the fact that since the seminal work of Akerlof (1970), limited econometric literature that attempts to estimate these models exist structurally. In a similar vein to d'Haultfoeuille and Février (2007), we could find no literature that attempts to explain the effects of artificial intelligence on the information asymmetries and, ultimately, the question of adverse selection, except the work by Marwala and Hurwitz (2017).

In the era of intense digitization, various business activities, including companies' business models (BMs) will be impacted. This era will be accompanied by and will enable various new forms of cooperation between economic agents. This is likely going to lead to new product and service offerings. The era of intense automation and digitization is likely going to push economic agents to some new forms of relationships. This could include sharing certain information that opens the opportunity for harvesting and storing big data that could be useful to economic agents, thus reducing the extent of adverse selection.

One of the advantages of intelligent agents is their updateability and connectivity (Harari, 2018). In the context of harvested and stored large data sets, intelligent agents linked (connected) to the data repositories would be updated on an ongoing basis as the new data is being captured. In our example of a dealership in Gezina that would have purchased a damaged accident car without having prior knowledge of this could pick up crucial information through big data and intelligent systems, allowing the dealership access to the information that would have been obscure to them.

In conclusion, we are of the view that AI brings the possibility of building, linking and analysing big data sets that would otherwise be impossible for a human being. This is because intelligent machines can process huge amounts of data, whether in a structured or unstructured format. The Institute of Chartered Accountants of England and Wales (2018) have argued that intelligent machines could process this data far much more than humans ever would. What makes intelligent machines more suitable for production floors is the fact that they can pick up weaker or more complex patterns in data than we can (The Institute of Chartered Accountants of England and Wales 2018). As such, the Institute suggests that intelligent machines may be better in environments that we find less predictable.

One other advantage of intelligent machines in the context of the production floor is that they can be far more consistent decision-makers. They do not suffer from tiredness or boredom (The Institute of Chartered Accountants of England and Wales 2018), which could be fatal in hazardous environments such as mining and quarrying.

As we move to the era of updateability and connectivity, the era that will be characterized by artificial intelligence, whichMarwala (2018) view as a computational technique for building machines that are intelligent, and which has in the past been used successfully to model complex problems, the rise and improvements, in AI has a potential to reduce asymmetric information, allowing economic agents to make decisions on the basis of near-complete information.

8.6 Key Points

- A wide range of literature has been devoted to understanding the consequences of the concept of information asymmetries.
- Economics, risk management and insurance are disciplines that employ both the concepts of moral hazard and adverse selection.
- Adverse selection occurs when one agent in a transaction has more information than the other party, thus giving it an advantage.
- Most information in a market-driven economy is transmitted through pricing, adverse selection will result in unfair pricing of goods and services and the unfair advantage on the part of the counterparty with more information.
- Certain scholars have suggested that there should be penalties or incentives so that transparent behaviour is promoted to limit the agency problem.
- It is clear that the action whether to disclose material facts or not is still dependent on one economic agent, which is expected to be unlikely in a situation where the disclosure of such information has a potential to reduce economic benefits to that particular economic agent.
- To address challenges similar to what Akerlof raised, the IAS Conceptual Framework would respond by stating that the disclosure and making available relevant information (financial information in thse context of the IAS) can make a difference in the decisions making process.
- The IAS Conceptual Framework appears to be appealing to the conscience or ethics that economic agents should do what is morally correct. This is clear from the use of the word "fair".
- One of the advantages of intelligent agents is their updateability and connectivity.
- Artificial intelligence has the potential to reduce asymmetric information, allowing economic agents to make decisions on the basis of near-complete information.

References

Akerlof G (1970) The market for 'lemons': quality uncertainty and the market mechanism. Quart J Econ 84(3):488–500

Almeida BJM (2014) The agency theory: the main foundational base to explain the auditing in Portuguese investor-oriented firms. Br J Econ Manag Trade 4(2):275–304

Belli P (2001) How adverse selection affects the health insurance market. Policy research working paper series 2574. The World Bank

d'Haultfoeuille X, Février P (2007) Identification and estimation of incentive problems: adverse selection. https://cowles.yale.edu/sites/default/files/files/conf/2008/sum_fevrier.pdf. Accessed 5 Mar 2019

Diamond P (1998) Optimal income taxation: an example with a U-shaped pattern of optimal marginal tax rates. Am Econ Rev 88:83–95

Eisenhardt MK (1989) Agency theory: an assessment and review. Academy of management review. Sage, London

Freixas X, Rochet JC (1997) The microeconomics of banking: microeconomics of banking. MIT Press, Boston, MA

Harari YN (2018) 21 lessons for the 21st century. Jonathan Cape, London

International Accounting Standards (2010) Conceptual framework for financial reporting 2010. https://www.iasplus.com/en/standards/other/framework. Accessed 2 Mar 2019

Jensen M, Meckling W (1976) Theory of a firm: managerial behaviour, agency costs and ownership structure. J Econ 3:305–360

Laffont JJ, Tirole J (1993) A theory of incentives in procurement and regulation. MIT Press, Boston, MA

Leke CA, Marwala T (2019) Deep learning and missing data in engineering systems. Springer, London. ISBN: 978-3030011796

Marwala T (2007) Computational intelligence for modelling complex systems. Research India Publications, Delhi

Marwala T (2009) Computational intelligence for missing data imputation, estimation, and management: knowledge optimization techniques. IGI Global, Pennsylvania

Marwala T (2010) Finite element model updating using computational intelligence techniques: applications to structural dynamics. Springer, Heidelberg

Marwala T (2013) Economic modeling using artificial intelligence methods. Springer, Heidelberg

Marwala T (2014) Artificial intelligence techniques for rational decision making. Springer, Heidelberg

Marwala T (2015) Causality, correlation, and artificial intelligence for rational decision making. World Scientific, Singapore

Marwala T (2018) Handbook of machine learning: foundation of artificial intelligence. World Scientific Publication

Marwala T, Hurwitz E (2017) Artificial intelligence and economic theory: skynet in the market. Springer. ISBN: 978-3-319-66103-2

Marwala T, Lagazio M (2011) Militarized conflict modeling using computational intelligence. Springer, Heidelberg

Marwala T, Boulkaibet I, Adhikari S (2017) Probabilistic finite element model updating using bayesian statistics: applications to aeronautical and mechanical engineering. Wiley, The Ultrium, Southern Gate, Chichester, West Sussex

Moloi T (2009) Assessment of corporate governance reporting in the annual report of South African listed companies. Masters dissertation, University of South Africa

Moloi T, Adelowotan M (2018) Exploring the risks disclosed in South African technical vocational education and training colleges' annual reports. S Afr J Account Audit Res 20:115–122

Stiglitz JE, Weiss A (1981) Credit rationing in markets with imperfect information. Am Econ Rev 3:393–410

The Institute of Chartered Accountants of England and Wales (2018) Artificial intelligence and the future of accountancy. ICAEW Thought Leadership, I.T. Faculty, United Kingdom

Tiessen P, Waterhouse JH (1983) Towards a descriptive theory of management accounting. J Account 3:251–267

Wilson R (1993) Nonlinear pricing. Oxford University Press, Oxford

Xing B, Marwala T (2018a) Smart computing applications in crowdfunding. CRC Press (Taylor and Francis), Routledge, London

Xing B, Marwala T (2018b) Smart maintenance for human–robot interaction: an intelligent search algorithmic perspective. Springer, London

Chapter 9
Moral Hazard

9.1 Introduction

The previous chapter discussed the concept of adverse selection, which is a problem that stems from information asymmetry, where a strategic behaviour by the more informed counterparty in a contract works against the interest of the less informed counterparties. In order to be in a position to place adverse selection in the context of artificial intelligence, two critical ways in which management and commerce studies have suggested to manage adverse selection are discussed, and this is the accounting framework and the agency theory.

In this chapter, we discuss the moral hazard theory in the context of artificial intelligence. This is to say that in the era of intense automation and digitization, we have the expectations that economic agents could form new frontiers of relationships. New frontiers could include, among other things, sharing information that would subsequently open opportunities for harvesting and storing big data that could be useful to all economic agents. In this era, what will become of the moral hazard theory?

We have suggested in chap. 8 of this book that AI brings the possibility of building, linking and analysing big data sets that would otherwise be impossible for a human being, thus reducing the extent of adverse selection. If adverse selection, as we have suggested in chap. 8, occurs when there is a lack of symmetric information before a deal between economic agents (Investopedia 2019), then the era of intense automation and digitization, to a certain degree could mitigate this.

What will then become of moral hazard theory? We restate the point made in chap. 8 that economics, risk management and insurance are disciplines that employ both the concepts of moral hazard and adverse selection (Akerlof 1970). Moral hazard occurs when one economic agent in a transaction decides to utilize the information advantage at their disposal to the detriment of the counterparty in the transaction. In the adverse selection, one party would only have had more information than the other party, thus giving it an advantage.

T. Moloi and T. Marwala, *Artificial Intelligence in Economics and Finance Theories*, Advanced Information and Knowledge Processing,
https://doi.org/10.1007/978-3-030-42962-1_9

The similarity between adverse selection and moral hazard is that both involve the information gap between two economic agents in the transaction. At the same time, the difference between adverse selection and moral hazard is that rather than one party in the transaction having the strategic advantage because of the information gap, the party with more information would use it to strategically position itself (strategic behaviour) against the interest of the less informed counterparty in a transaction (Belli 2001) and to the detriment of the less informed party. What we see from the moral hazard theory is that while it also stems from information asymmetry, where a strategic behaviour by the more informed counterparty in a contract works against the interest of the less informed counterparties (Akerlof 1970; Almeida 2014; Belli 2001), like its counterpart, the adverse selection, it is clear that one party would not have entered into the transaction in good faith.

Similarly to chap. 8, in this chapter we examine how the moral theory will look like in a situation where the information is produced and stored by the intelligent systems, and a scenario where the information is digitally available and easily accessible to all parties in the transaction. This is an era characterized by the rise of the machine through artificial intelligence. It is also an era that brings along it an advent of cyber-physical systems representing new ways in which technology becomes embedded within societies, i.e. business, government, civil society, etc., and the human body. It is driven by the rapid convergence of advanced technologies across the biological, physical and digital worlds. This era is said to be marked by emerging technology breakthroughs in several fields, including robotics, artificial intelligence, biotechnology, etc. All of these breakthroughs have come with unique impacts on every aspect of human lives, including business (Harari 2018; Agrawal et al. 2018; Marwala and Hurwitz 2017).

9.2 Moral Hazard

In defining moral hazard, The Economic Times (2019) views it as "a situation in which one party gets involved in a risky event knowing that it is protected against the risk and the other party will incur the cost. It arises when both the parties have incomplete information about each other". This definition is consistent with our explanation of the concept in the earlier sections, where we explained that both adverse selection and moral hazard emanate from the information gap between two economic agents in the transaction. The party with the information advantage could decide to utilize the information advantage at their disposal to the detriment of the counterparty in the transaction.

In revisiting our earliest example used in chap. 8, we used Gezina (an area that is in Tshwane, formerly known as Pretoria, the administrative capital of South Africa) which is the area that is full of second-hand (used) motor vehicle dealerships, and we sought to explain Akerlof's (1970) logic of asymmetric information. In this example, we supposed that one of these dealerships has two similar-looking cars and the difference between these two cars is the way in which the previous owners would have handled them. In our supposition, one of the cars would have been well handled. This car would have been properly taken care of, i.e. serviced at the right intervals. The second car, however, would not have been well looked after. In this regard, the previous owner would not have maintained (serviced) the car at the right intervals. Several service appointments were missed. Further, it had damage to the rear bumper, which was later fixed, effectively making it an accident damaged vehicle.

In selling the cars to the dealerships, the previous owner of "the damaged" vehicle did not disclose its previous condition. We suppose that the dealership secured these two motor vehicles for R100 000 each ($7142 each). Had the dealership known that one of the vehicles is an accident damaged vehicle, it would not have paid R100 000. It would have paid far much less than what it paid. The lack of information in the accident and not correctly serviced car has undermined the decision-making of this dealership. Akerlof (1970) refers to this as market failure and a classic case of adverse selection.

In line with our explanation of moral hazard earlier, one party with the information advantage, in this regard the owner of "the damaged" vehicle would have decided to utilize the information advantage at their disposal to the detriment of the counterparty in the transaction, the second-hand dealership.

If we suppose that the "the damaged" vehicle is later sold to the dealership's client without the problems being identified, and later the client's dealership identifies problems, which point out that this was in fact a "damaged" vehicle from the onset, the dealership could be forced to refund the client, and get its reputation damaged, and which could impact on its goodwill.

Essentially, the question of information gap follows a three-step approach which could be graphically presented as follows:

Figure 9.1 above essentially explains that there is a three-step process in the information gap. The first step is that one economic agent could seek to hold a strategic information advantage of its counterparties in the transaction. If the economic agent behaves in this manner, she or he will cause her or his counterparties to enter into a transaction they would not have entered had they been provided with the total picture. Once the transaction is entered into, and there is an agreement, the economic agent holding some information will now have the strategic information advantage over her or his counterparties. If the economic agent uses this information to the detriment of the other counterparties interested, then the moral hazard occurs.

9.3 Adverse Selection, Moral Hazard and the Agency Problem

In chap. 8, we highlighted that the typical finance and accounting literature has responded to the situation by suggesting the agency theory and attempting to mitigate agency problems. To recap this discussion, Moloi (2009) notes that in *The Theory of the Firm*, Jensen and Meckling (1976) examined the relationship between principals

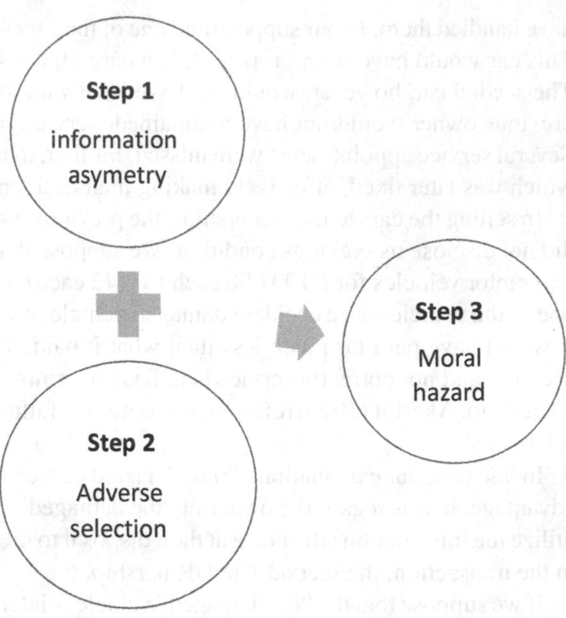

Fig. 9.1 The three-step approach of information gap. *Source* Authors' own conceptualisation

and agents in a company, which culminated in the proposal of the theory of the firm that was based on conflicts of interest between various contracting parties, namely, shareholders, managers and debtholders.

The relationship characterized by conflicting interests between shareholders, managers and debtholders is referred to as the agency theory (Moloi 2009). According to Moloi (2009) citing Eisenhardt (1989), this is "the ever-present agency relationship in companies, where one party (the principal) delegates work to another (the agent), who has to perform that work, i.e. the principal mandates the agent to do a specific task and the agent is remunerated for that task".

Under conditions of imperfect information and uncertainty as demonstrated in Fig. 9.1, "which is the situation in most companies, because of the complex shareholding, for example, in public companies, two agency problems arise, and that is the adverse selection and moral hazard" (Moloi 2009; Eisenhardt 1989).

As explained by Moloi (2009), "the first problem arises when the desires or goals of the principal and agent conflict, and it is difficult or expensive for the principal to verify what the agent is doing. The problem here is that the principal cannot verify that the agent has behaved appropriately". Eisenhardt (1989) refers to this situation as an adverse selection.

Once more, Moloi (2009), citing Eisenhardt (1989), explains the second problem, that the agency problem occurs in the way that it "arises when both the principal and agent have different attitudes towards risk. The problem here is that the principal and the agent may prefer different actions because of their differing risk preferences. This is known as moral hazard".

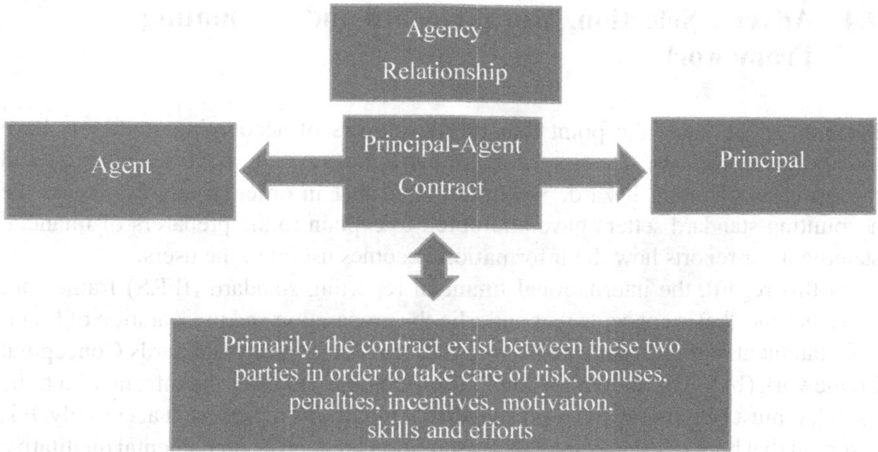

Fig. 9.2 The agency relationship. *Source* Moloi (2009)—information was sourced from Tiessen and Waterhouse (1983: 251–267)

In order to mitigate the agency problem, which results in adverse selection and, subsequently, to the moral hazard, Tiessen and Waterhouse (1983) suggest that there should be penalties or incentives so that transparent behaviour is promoted. Figure 9.2 demonstrate the agency relationship and how the relationship between the agent and principal is managed.

If we were to follow Tiessen and Waterhouse's (1983) suggestion, and using our example of a dealership in Gezina, what this means is that the seller of an accident damaged motor vehicle could be charged with misrepresentation for not disclosing material information. Similarly, the seller could be incentivized if they disclose all material information regarding the condition of the motor vehicle.

From this discussion, we made a point that penalties and incentives do not resolve the question of asymmetric information, adverse selection and, subsequently, the question of the moral hazard. In our view, the reason this solution would have difficulties in mitigating asymmetric information, adverse selection, and the question of the moral hazard lies in the fact that the decision whether to disclose material facts or not is dependent on one economic agent. If this agent is of the view that they could gain some advantage over their counterparties, in our view, it will be unlikely that there will be a disclosure of such information.

We made a point in chap. 8 that the disclosure of such information could have a detrimental effect on the economic agent that has it, and would have the potential to reduce economic benefits to that particular economic agent. What the agency theory and the proposed solutions to the agency problems are asking economic agents to do is that they should regulate their behaviour. It assumes that incentives could persuade economic agents into disclosing material information or that the agents could be coerced by threats of penalties.

9.4 Adverse Selection, Moral Hazard and Accounting Framework

In chap. 8, we made the point that the developers of accounting standards have also grappled with the question of asymmetric information, adverse selection and the question of moral hazard. We highlighted that in order to address these, the accounting standard setters have attempted to explain to the preparers of financial statements or reports how the information becomes useful to the users.

In this regard, the international financial reporting standard (IFRS) framework describes the "basic concepts that underlie the preparation and presentation of financial statements for external users" (International Accounting Standards Conceptual Framework (IAS) (2010); Moloi and Adelowotan (2018)). For the information to be useful, it must be relevant and represents what it purports to represent accurately. It is essential that both relevance and fair presentation are seen as fundamental qualitative characteristics.

We noted in chap. 8 that the IAS is convinced that once the information is relevant and fairly presented, it could then be useful to the decision-making. Further, we highlighted that the IAS (2010) is of the view "that the usefulness of financial information is enhanced if it is comparable, verifiable, timely, and understandable". These four factors were described in detail in chap. 8 of this book.

Our observation made in the conditions of adverse selection still holds even under the conditions of moral hazard. We observed that the main difficulty with the IAS (2010) framework is that economic agents in the transaction have a divergent interest. We reiterate the same conditions here that one party in a transaction would always have a piece of better information than the other party. Going back to the example of our dealership in Gezina, the owner of the accident damaged car has a piece of better knowledge about the problems of the motor vehicle than the dealership to which the motor vehicle was subsequently sold.

We made the point in chap. 8 that what the IAS is asking that the economic agent should work against maximizing what he/she could potentially receive as the proceeds of the sale of the motor vehicle to the dealership if this information was to be kept by him/her. Our view in this regard is that the IAS (2010) appears to be appealing to the conscience or ethics that economic agents should do what is morally correct. This is clear from the use of the word "fair". Similarly to the agency theory and the agency problem, the IAS assumes that economic agents could be persuaded to be fair by disclosing material information, which could be detrimental to them and to the benefit of the counterparties in the transaction.

9.5 Artificial Intelligence, Adverse Selection and Moral Hazard

We draw the same conclusions similar to those that we put forward in the discussion of adverse selection. We think AI brings the possibility of building, linking and analysing big data sets that would otherwise be impossible for a human being. As we move to the era of updateability and connectivity, the era that will be characterized by artificial intelligence, which Marwala (2018) views as a computational technique for building machines that are intelligent, the rise and improvements in AI have a potential to reduce asymmetric information. This allows economic agents to make decisions on the basis of near-complete information.

From this perspective, we are of the view that AI will outperform the mitigation actions put forward by the finance and accounting literature, the agency theory and the conceptual framework. With AI, there is no need to rely on the economic agents to be "fair" by disclosing material information. There is also no need to persuade economic agents with incentives for disclosing material information or coercing them with threats of penalties. The era of intense automation and digitization is likely going to push economic agents to some new forms of relationships. This could include sharing certain information that opens the opportunity for harvesting and storing big data that could be useful to economic agents, thus reducing the extent of adverse selection.

With their advantage, namely, updateability and connectivity (Harari 2018), intelligent agents will be swift in picking up information discrepancies. Perhaps, knowing that intelligent agents are widely deployed, and that data is harvested from different repositories which could be accessed by the click of the button, economic agents would volunteer the material data. The volunteered information could, in any case, have been stored, which will make the volunteering process a confirmatory process.

9.6 Key Points

- We examine two ways in which management literature has suggested to manage asymmetric information, adverse selection and moral hazard by examining the accounting framework and the agency theory.
- The conceptual framework assumes that economic agents could be persuaded to be fair by disclosing material information, which could be detrimental to them and to the benefit of the counterparties in the transaction.
- The agency theory assumes that incentives could persuade economic agents to disclose material information, or they could be coerced to do this through threats of penalties.
- With their advantage, namely, updateability and connectivity, intelligent agents will be swift in picking up information discrepancies.

- AI brings the possibility of building, linking and analysing big data sets that would otherwise be impossible for a human being.
- AI will outperform the mitigation actions put forward by the finance and accounting literature, the agency theory and the conceptual framework.
- With AI, there is no need to rely on the economic agents to be "fair" by disclosing material information.
- As AI advances, we also do not think there will be need to persuade economic agents through incentives of disclosing material information or coercing them by threats of penalties.

References

Agrawal A, Gans J, Goldfarb A (2018) Prediction machines: the simple economics of artificial intelligence. Harvard Business Review Press, Boston, Massachusetts

Akerlof G (1970) The market for 'lemons': quality uncertainty and the market mechanism. Q J Econ 84(3):488–500

Almeida BJM (2014) The agency theory: the main foundational base to explain the auditing in Portuguese investor-oriented firms. Br J Econ Manage Trade 4(2):275–304

Belli P (2001). How adverse selection affects the health insurance market. Policy research working paper series 2574. The World Bank

Eisenhardt MK (1989) Agency theory: an assessment and review. academy of management review. SAGE, London

Harari YN (2018) 21 lessons for the 21st century. Jonathan Cape, London

International Accounting Standards (2010). Conceptual framework for financial reporting 2010. Retrieved 2 March, 2019, from https://www.iasplus.com/en/standards/other/framework

Investopedia (2019) Moral Hazard. Retrieved 2 March, 2019, from https://www.investopedia.com/terms/m/moralhazard.asp

Jensen M, Meckling W (1976) Theory of a firm: managerial behaviour, agency costs and ownership structure. J Econ 3:305–360

Marwala T (2018) Handbook of machine learning: foundation of artificial intelligence. World Scientific Publication

Marwala T, Hurwitz E (2017) Artificial intelligence and economic theory: skynet in the market. Springer

Moloi T, Adelowotan M (2018) Exploring the risks disclosed in South African technical vocational education and training colleges' annual reports. S Afr J Account Audit Res 20:115–122

Moloi T (2009) Assessment of corporate governance reporting in the annual report of South African listed companies. Masters dissertation, University of South Africa

Tiessen P, Waterhouse JH (1983) Towards a descriptive theory of management accounting. J Account 3:251–267

The Economic Times (2019) Definition of Moral Hazard. Retrieved 04 April, 2019, from https://economictimes.indiatimes.com/definition/moral-hazard

Chapter 10
Creative Destruction

10.1 Introduction

According to Schumpeter (1942), creative destruction is defined as "the process by which information and communication technology destroys previous technological solutions and lays waste old companies in order to make room for the new companies". Google has replaced recent search engines to become the largest search engine worldwide.

Interestingly, Marwala (2019) points out that Google has become the most extensive library, even though it does not own any physical library. It has managed to do this by using the index that takes customers to their desired websites. Scholars such as Nietzsche (2003) and Reinert and Reinert (2006) are of the view that the emergence of new technology, in our example Google, is not at all the wrong thing. They propose that the destruction of old technology and its replacement with a new one is necessary in order to avoid stagnation.

Paragraphs below will provide a brief overview of the concept of creative destruction; this will be followed by a discussion on creative destruction and artificial intelligence. Finally, we will outline the key points around creative destruction and artificial intelligence.

10.2 Creative Destruction

In his book titled "Capitalism, socialism and democracy", Joseph Schumpeter popularized the creative destruction theory as a theory concerned with two things, namely, innovation and the business cycle. Schumpeter derived the theory from the work of Karl Marx. According to Schumpeter (1942), the "gale of creative destruction" can be described as the "process of industrial mutation that incessantly revolutionizes the economic structure from within, incessantly destroying the old one [while at the same time it] incessantly creating a new one".

T. Moloi and T. Marwala, *Artificial Intelligence in Economics and Finance Theories*, Advanced Information and Knowledge Processing,
https://doi.org/10.1007/978-3-030-42962-1_10

The concept of gale destruction refers more broadly to the linked processes of the accumulation and annihilation of wealth under capitalism (Schumpeter 1994; Schumpeter 1942). Sidak et al. (2009) have reinterpreted the work of Schumpeter. In their reinterpretation, they posit that in Schumpeter's vision of capitalism, innovative entry by entrepreneurs was the disruptive force that sustained economic growth, even as it destroyed the value of established companies and "labourers that enjoyed some degree of monopoly power derived from previous technological", organizational, regulatory and economic paradigms (Sidak et al. 2009).

Antonelli (2003) points out that the crucial aspect to the Schumpeterian insight is the idea of innovations. Accordingly, this idea implies that the concept of creative destruction is synonymous with the innovative process. In essence, their argument is that this has all to do with a process of bringing up new technology, which effectively renders the previous one useless innovative.

In line with the above, Antonelli (2003) points out that it is an innovation that most economists believe is a primary driver of economic growth in today's knowledge-based economy. In essence, what this means is that it is not capital accumulation as neoclassical economics asserts that grows the economy, but innovative capacity spurred by appropriable knowledge and technological externalities. This is consistent with Schumpeter's suggestion that economic cycles are primarily the consequence of innovation. Further, Schumpeter had suggested that innovative activities and innovative organizations are re-shaped by economic crises (Ciborowski 2016).

Antonelli (2003) acknowledges that economic growth in innovation economics is the end-product of:

- knowledge (tacit versus codified);
- regimes and policies allowing for entrepreneurship and innovation;
- technological spill overs and externalities between collaborative firms and
- systems of innovation that create innovative environments.

These points are in line with Schumpeter's (1942) claim that growth in a market economy could only be sustained through radical innovations (creative destruction) by entrepreneurs, which allows them to outcompete and destroy existing firms and monopolies, frequently leading to new temporary monopolies destined to succumb to future radical innovations. In providing an example of the above, Schumpeter (1941) used "the railroadization of the Middle West". Schumpeter (1941) writes that; "the Illinois Central not only meant very good business while it was built and while new cities were built around it and land was cultivated, but it spelled the death sentence for the [old] agriculture of the West".

Even today, we see the same trends taking place across the world in the sense that "companies that once revolutionized and dominated new industries—for example, Xerox in copiers or Polaroid in instant photography—have seen their profits fall and their dominance vanish as rivals launched improved designs or cut manufacturing costs. In technology, the cassette tape replaced the 8-track, only to be replaced in turn by the compact disc, which was undercut by downloads to MP3 players, which is now being usurped by web-based streaming services" (The Guardian 2015).

Archibugi (2016) points to the fact that innovations do not have an economic impact in isolation; they become dominant because they are applied in different contexts, shaping and transforming original ideas. Accordingly, "innovations could occur in different economic arenas (e.g. steam engines and textile machinery), but they are mixed and recombined in the economic and social fabric (e.g. the steam engine provided power for textile mills)" (Archibugi 2016).

Further, Archibugi (2016) observes that "when the new knowledge associated with a few emerging technologies starts to become widely diffused in economic life, then it will generate a phase of economic expansion". In this regard, "new technological opportunities stimulate and open up new industries that did not exist before, leading to job creation and structural change". Having said this, Archibugi (2016) points out that when opportunities "start to dry up, it is likely that there will be a lower rate of economic growth or even an economic crisis".

The view above is consistent with Schumpeter's suggestion "that economic cycles are the consequence of innovation, but also that innovative activities and innovative organizations are re-shaped by economic crises" (Ciborowski 2016).

10.3 Creative Destruction Theory and Artificial Intelligence

In 1973, Bell wrote in "The Coming of Post-Industrial Society" that the leading product would change from being goods to being information (Bell 1973). Marwala (2019) makes the similar point in his work titled "Data is the new Gold". Accordingly, he writes that "the idea of gold as the most important economic asset has passed. Instead of entrepreneurs going to California to look for gold, as they did in the past, they now go to Silicon Valley to create companies that exploit the acquisition and sharing of data" (Marwala 2019).

Given that companies such as those that we mentioned above would have had enormous data of people that use them, we think that with the AI-powered analytics the idea of creative destruction as espoused by Schumpeter would hold as far as technology is concerned. However, companies that would be pioneers of the time may not necessarily fold and close doors. Schumpeter viewed creative destruction as the process by which new information and communication technology destroys previous technological solutions and lays waste old companies in order to make room for the new companies.

Basic analytics packages that were used then by most organizations could be argued as having been a possible tip of an iceberg. In a sense, they couldn't provide deep insights about the organizations true state of affairs. We argue that the concept of a tip of an iceberg was also true even on reports around what had happened and why it happened. This, during the heydays of companies such as HotBot, Excite, WebCrawler, Ask Jeeves, Ask.com, Yahoo, Go.com, Netscape, Dogpile, AltaVista, ananzi, Lycos, MSN Search, Bing, AOL Search, Infoseek, MetaCrawler, was so because of troves and troves of data that organizational stakeholders, particularly customers, generated, but could not be entirely analysed.

The advent of the Internet of Things meant that data was now generated through different channels because of the Internet of Things devices. We hypothesize that companies that fell victim to the gayle of destruction had no capacity to analyse and understand the large portion of their data, such as what customers are looking for and the future in general. In essence, these companies may not necessarily have been prepared to use data at their disposal to advance compelling experiences on every channel that delighted their customers and exceeded their highest expectations, which would have allowed them to move with times.

Large amounts of data brought about by the advent of the Internet of Things can mean that there are plenty of insights that companies that were affected by the gayle of destruction rarely knew existed. We think, as a result of this, these companies could not take advantage of their position in the market. They could not understand their market and where their market was headed.

The advantage of companies such as Google, Facebook and Uber is that they are already deploying AI in their data analytics in order to source new business opportunities and stay ahead. In a study that MIT Sloan conducted, it appears that there is an agreement that companies that deploy AI will be in a position to gain insight of the market and where the market is headed, which will allow them to react accordingly. The MIT Sloan study found that almost 85% of senior executives surveyed across the world "believed that AI will allow their companies to obtain or sustain a competitive advantage" (Ransbotham et al. 2017).

Marwala (2019) analyses three companies that have succesfully deployed AI in order to take advantage of the fingerprints (which is data) that customers leave as they use these company services.

- He writes that "facebook's most valuable asset is not the software that connects people, which can easily be replicated, but the data of the over two billion active users it connects".
- Similarly, he observes that the "most valuable asset of Uber, the ride-hailing service that does not own a single taxi, is the data of the people who use it".
- Finally, "the prime asset of Google, the largest library, which owns no physical library, is the index that takes customers to their desired websites".

Since data is the new gold, we think that companies that take advantage of AI for the purpose of advanced data analytics would be able to deploy this for the purpose of analysing large amounts of data brought about the advent of the Internet of Things.

This, we hypothesize, can mean that there are plenty of insights for those companies in the coalface, the gayle of destruction in this regard will not bring about new entrepreneurs or new companies but the same companies, and insights from data and predictive analytics will show them which technology is to be destroyed and what it needs to be replaced with. Whatever the replacement will be, it will be based on troves of data that allows these companies and gives them the competitive advantage to understand their market and where their market is headed.

10.4 Key Points

- Entrepreneurs are no longer "going to California to look for gold, as they did in the past; they now go to Silicon Valley to create companies that exploit the acquisition and sharing of data".
- Large amounts of data brought about by the advent of the Internet of Things can mean that there are plenty of insights that companies that were affected by the gayle of destruction rarely knew it existed.
- Companies that are in the coalface would have had enormous data of people that use it; we think that with the AI-powered analytics, the idea of creative destruction as espoused by Schumpeter would hold as far as technology is concerned; however, companies that would be pioneers of the time may not necessarily fold and close doors.
- Since data is the new gold, we think that companies that take advantage of AI for the purpose of advanced data analytics would be able to deploy this for the purpose of analysing large amounts of data brought about by the advent of the Internet of Things.
- Our hypothesis is that the above can only mean that there are plenty of insights for those companies in the coalface, the gayle of destruction in this regard will not bring about new entrepreneurs or new companies but the same companies and insights from data, and predictive analytics will show them which technology is to be destroyed and what it needs to be replaced with. Whatever replacement there will be, it will be based on troves of data, which gives these companies the competitive advantage to understand their market and where their market is headed.

References

Antonelli C (2003) The economics of innovation, new technologies, and structural change. Routledge, London

Archibugi D (2016) Blade runner economics: will innovation lead the economic recovery? Res Policy. https://doi.org/10.1016/j.respol.2016.01.021

Bell D (1973) The coming of post-industrial society. Basic Books, New York

Ciborowski R (2016) Innovation systems in the terms of Schumpeterian creative destruction. Econ Econom Financ 4:29–37. https://doi.org/10.21303/2504-5571.2016.00114

Marwala T (2019) Data is new gold. Retrieved 03 Dec, 2019, from https://www.forbesafrica.com/technology/2019/07/18/data-is-the-new-gold/

Nietzsche F (2003) Thus spake Zarathustra: A book for all and none. Translation from German by Thomas Wayne. Algora Publishing, New York

Ransbotham S, Kiron D, Gerbert P, Reeves M (2017) Reshaping business with artificial intelligence. MIT sloan management review. Retrieved 04 Dec 12 2019, from https://sloanreview.mit.edu/projects/reshaping-business-with-artificial-intelligence/

Reinert H, Reinert ES (2006) Creative destruction in economics: Nietzsche, Sombart, Schumpeter. In: Backhaus JG, Drechsler W (eds) Friedrich Nietzsche (1844–1900). The European heritage in economics and the social sciences, vol 3. Springer, Boston, MA

Schumpeter JA (1994) [1942] Capitalism, socialism and democracy. Harper and Brothers, United States of America, New York

Schumpeter JA (1941) An economic interpretation of our time: the lowell lectures, in the economics and sociology of capitalism, Princeton NJ, Princeton University Press, pp 349. (As quoted by Andersen ES, Schumpeter and Regional Innovation. In: Cooke P (ed) Chapter for Handbook of Regional Innovation and Growth. Elgar Publishing)

Sidak J, Gregory T, David J (2009) Dynamic competition in antitrust law. J Compet Law Econ 5(4): 581–631. https://doi.org/10.1093/joclec/nhp024

Schwartz B (2009) A look back at the old search engines. Retrieved 03 Dec, 2019, from https://searchengineland.com/a-look-back-at-the-old-search-engines-25766

The Guardian (2015) Warner music streaming income overtaken by download. The Guardian, Tuesday 12 May 2015

Chapter 11
The Agency Theory

11.1 Introduction

Kopp (2019) views the agency theory as a principle utilized in an attempt to explain the complicated relationship that exists between the owners (principal) and managers (agents) of the business. Jensen and Meckling popularized this theory in their 1976 seminal work. In this work, they defined the agency relationship as "a form of contract between a company's owners and its managers, where the owners (as principal) appoint an agent (the managers) to manage the company on their behalf". The agency relationship is commonly found between shareholders (also known as principals) and company executives (also known as agents).

Other similar relationships depict the agency relationship, for instance, the relationship between financial planners and portfolio managers (agents) and investors (principals). A further example of the agency relationship will be that of a lessor and a lessee. In this example, a lessee is an agent, and a lessor is a principal. The relationship will be complicated when the goals of the agent and those of the principal are not congruent, which yields the agency problem. In the era dominated by intelligent machines, we expect that the agency theory will be affected.

According to Kaplan Publishing (2018), some key concepts assist in illustrating the agency theory. We discuss these concepts below:

- Firstly, it includes the fact that an agent is a person employed by a principal, with responsibility for carrying out a task on the principal's behalf.
- Secondly, the term agency would ordinarily refer to the existing relationship between a business owner and the organization's management.
- Thirdly, the agency costs would refer to those costs that are incurred by principals in an effort to monitor agency behaviour. This occurs because the agent may lack good faith due to self-interest.
- Fourthly, the concept of the agency loss, which would refer to the losses that the principal will incur because of the actions of the agent. Teeboom (2018) is of the view that if the agent was to behave appropriately and in the interest of the

T. Moloi and T. Marwala, *Artificial Intelligence in Economics and Finance Theories*, Advanced Information and Knowledge Processing,
https://doi.org/10.1007/978-3-030-42962-1_11

principal, the agency loss will be zero. Contrary to this, if the agent misbehaves, and in his or her interest, then the agency loss will rise.

11.2 The Tenets of the Agency Theory

The agency theory reflects the ever-present relationship between the owners of capital (also known as principals) and those that are entrusted to manage that capital (also known as agents). In companies, the agency relationship will be demonstrated by the relationship between shareholders (principals) and company executives (also known as agents). In financial transactions, suppose the investment space, the relationship can be demonstrated by financial planners and portfolio managers acting as agents and investors acting as principals.

In the property market, the agency relationship could manifest in the lessor and a lessee transaction. In this example, a lessee is an agent, and a lessor is a principal. Using the explanation given by the Institute of Chartered Accountants in England and Wales ICAEW (2005), an agency relationship comes into existence the moment the owner of a business engages someone to act as their agent to carry out a duty in their place.

According to Kopp (2019), the agency problem arises from the situation that many decisions that affect the principal, financially or otherwise, are made by the agent. Due to differences in priorities and interests, agents can take excessive risks contrary to what the principal desires. Linder and Foss (2015) have argued that, in this manner, the agent would have misbehaved. What we are learning from Linder and Foss' (2015) argument is that the agency theory is based on the assumption that the interests of a principal and the agent are not always in alignment. From the discussion above, Mitnick (2006) has pointed out that in the past, experience has demonstrated that directors have not always acted in the shareholders' best interests.

As discussed in Chaps. 8 and 9, Moloi (2009) notes that in *The Theory of the Firm*, Jensen and Meckling (1976) examined the relationship between principals and agents in a company, which culminated in the proposal of the theory of the firm based upon conflicts of interest between various contracting parties, namely, shareholders, managers and debtholders.

As discussed in Chaps. 8 and 9, this relationship is graphically depicted as shown below.

As discussed in the early chapters, Moloi (2009) pointed out that the principal-agent contract exists in order to mitigate the agency problem. As noted, the first problem arises when the desires or goals of the principal and the actions and decisions of the agent conflict, and it is difficult or expensive for the principal to verify what the agent is doing. The problem here is that the principal cannot verify that the agent has behaved appropriately. Eisenhardt (1989) refers to this situation as adverse selection.

Once more, Moloi (2009) citing Eisenhardt (1989) explains the second problem, that the agency problem occurs in the way that it "arises when both the principal and agent have different attitudes towards risk. The problem here is that the principal and the agent may prefer different actions because of their different risk preferences. This is known as a moral hazard".

In order to mitigate the agency problem, which results in adverse selection and, subsequently, the moral hazard, Tiessen and Waterhouse (1983) suggest that there should be penalties or incentives so that transparent behaviour is promoted. Penalties and bonuses are mechanisms that are built into the contract in order to promote congruence or alignment in the principal's expectations and the agent's behaviour.

Under conditions of imperfect information, which is the situation in most companies because of the complex shareholding, ordinarily, two agency problems will arise; adverse selection and moral hazard (Moloi 2009; Eisenhardt 1989). A detailed discussion of both these theories was undertaken in Chaps. 8 and 9. In engaging in the agency relationship, the governance dictates are that the principal will delegate the authority to the agent. This implies that the principal would have to trust the agent, and we argue that he/she hopes that the agent, in undertaking his or her fiduciary duties will not contradict the interest of the principal (Panda and Leepsa 2017; Mitnick 2006).

In the introduction, we discussed the critical concepts of the agency theory as espoused by Kaplan Publishing (2018). We are of the view that this is a simplified version of the complicated agency relationship that, as we demonstrated in Fig. 11.1, may contain several variables. As indicated in the preceding sections, particularly in Fig. 11.1, modern companies are characterized by a complex structure of shareholding. As such, owners will delegate the day-to-day activities to management, which creates the agency problem (Linder and Foss 2015). Due to the nature of this complex structure, variables in the agency relationship are broader than what is described in the Kaplan Publishing concepts.

Were the Kaplan Publishing (2018) concepts of the agency theory to be accepted with all the shortcomings, graphically the critical concepts as espoused can be depicted as in Fig. 11.2.

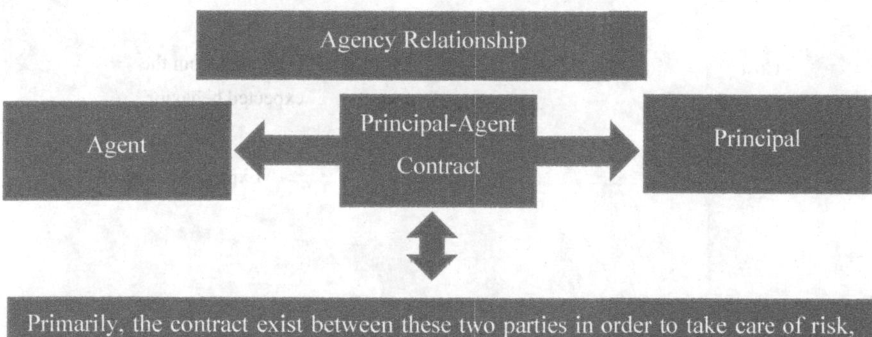

Fig. 11.1 The agency relationship. *Source* Moloi (2009)—information sourced from Tiessen and Waterhouse (1983, 251–267)

Fig. 11.2 Graphical depiction of Kaplan's suggested concepts of the agency theory

The fourth concept deals with the idea of the agency loss. For instance, suppose that the agent was to behave appropriately and in the interest of the principal, then the agency loss will be expected to be zero. In contrary, if the agent misbehaves, the agent, in a sense, begins to behave in his or her interest, leading to the rise of the agency loss.

In our view, what other literature has not sufficiently dealt with, which is essential and has been highlighted in Kaplan's Publishing (2018) is the relationship between behaviour and cost. We are expanding Kaplan's Publishing's (2018) proposition. We remodel this proposition and depict it using the curve. Accordingly, there exist two sets of behaviours that the principal ought to expect when engaging in the agency relationship. First, the agent can behave in the manner that is expected or the behaviour can deviate from the expected. We demonstrate this relationship using Fig. 11.3.

Figure 11.3 depicts two sets of behaviours that the principal ought to expect when engaging in the agency relationship. We have termed the first set of behaviour as

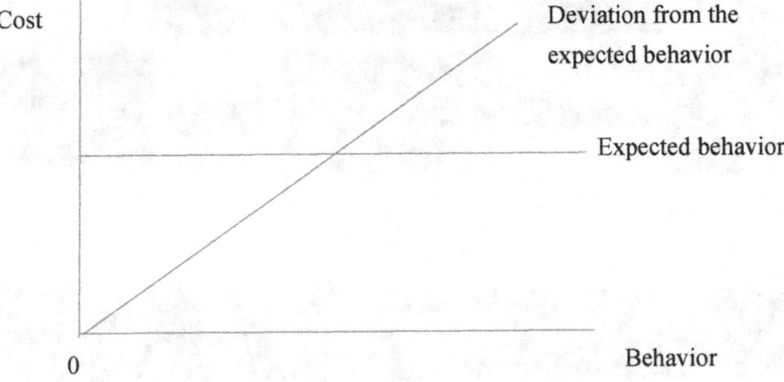

Fig. 11.3 Relationship between behaviour and cost

the idea that the agent can behave in a manner that the principal expects the agent to behave. We have further termed the second set of behaviour as the idea that the behaviour can deviate from the expected.

As can be seen in Fig. 11.3, should the agent behave in a manner that the principal expects the agent to behave, that is to say, the agent's priorities and interests are congruent with that of the principal, the agency cost will be zero. Our curve demonstrates that the moment the agent's priorities and interests deviate from the expected behaviour, the agency costs see incremental increases.

11.3 Artificial Intelligence and the Agency Theory

Given the fact that the agency theory is an attempt to explain the complexity of human behaviour in the principal-agent relationship, what happens to it in the era dominated by intelligent machines? We see this as an era dominated by intelligent machines, which is embedded on artificial intelligence. This is the world where digitization has led to most of our information fingerprints, personal and business being kept in large databases. This information is a significant source of both structured and unstructured data.

In this era, we are realizing the advent of cyber-physical systems, which represent new ways in which technology becomes embedded within societies, i.e. business, government, civil society, etc., and the human body; it is driven by the rapid convergence of advanced technologies across the biological, physical and digital worlds.

This era is said to be marked by emerging technology breakthroughs in several fields, including robotics, artificial intelligence, biotechnology, etc. All of these breakthroughs have come with unique impacts on every aspect of human lives, including business (Harari 2018; Agrawal et al. 2018; Marwala and Hurwitz 2017).

Our position is that in the context of artificial intelligence, where intense automation and digitization are orders of the day, we have expectations that economic agents could form new frontiers of relationships, which challenges the basis of the agency theory as we know it. The new frontiers that we are envisaging could include, among other things, the certainty of sharing of intelligent information that would, in the context of the agency theory, be available to both the agent and the principal.

In Chaps. 8 and 9, we outlined the advantages of intelligent systems as updateability and connectivity (Harari 2018). Using their strength, which lies in these two characteristics, we think intelligent agents will be swift in picking up the information discrepancies. Intelligent systems have the capability of harvesting information from different sources. Once gathered, this information will be updated in the principal's system, given that the systems will be integrated.

We have a similar conclusion as we had in Chaps. 8 and 9. The conclusion is that it is probable that perhaps the agent, knowing that intelligent agents are widely deployed and that these intelligent systems have the capability of harvesting data from different repositories, will moderate his or her behaviour to be closely aligned

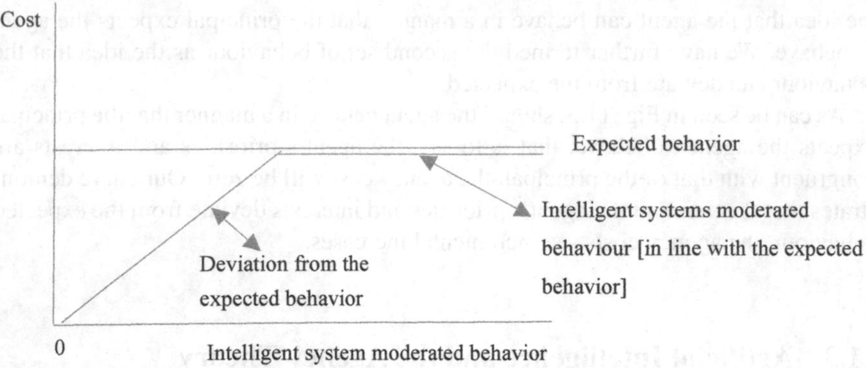

Fig. 11.4 Relationship between intelligent system moderated behaviour and cost

to that of the principal. Then, the cost associated with the misbehaviour will also moderate.

Figure 11.4 depicts three sets of behaviours with the introduction of AI-powered intelligent systems. The first two behaviours were discussed in Fig. 11.3. As can be noted in Fig. 11.4, before the introduction of AI-powered intelligent systems, if the agent's priorities and interests deviate from the expected behaviour, the agency costs saw incremental increases; however, the introduction of AI-powered intelligent systems moderates the behaviour to be in line with the expected behaviour.

We propose that the agents' behaviour will moderate due to, among other things, the fact that intelligent agents will be swift in picking up information discrepancies. Intelligent systems have the capability of harvesting information from different sources. Once gathered, this information will be updated in the principal's system, as the systems will be integrated.

The moderation also occurs because of new frontiers, which include, among other things, the certainty of sharing of intelligent information that, in the context of the agency theory, would be available to both the agent and the principal, reducing information asymmetry between these two economic agents. Finally, moderation could occur because the agent, knowing that intelligent agents are deployed widely and that these intelligent systems have the capability of harvesting data from different repositories, the agent will moderate his or her behaviour to be closely aligned with that of the principal.

11.4 Key Points

- The agency theory attempts to explain the complicated relationship that exists between the owners (principal) and managers (agents) of the business.

- Because the owners of capital delegate the decision-making relating to their capital to agents, it is given that agents will have more information compared to the owners. This situation creates information asymmetry.
- Agents can use the information at their disposal in order to make decisions that are not congruent to those of the principal.
- To manage this complicated relationship, and to attempt to align the desires and goals of both parties, a contract forms the basis of this relationship.
- Even with the existence of the contract, the problem associated with asymmetric information is not eliminated.
- The principal will take additional steps in an attempt to manage the behaviour of the agent. The attempt to manage the behaviour of the agent has its associated costs.
- When the desires or goals of the principal and agent conflict, it is difficult or expensive for the principal to verify what the agent is doing.
- With AI, we are envisaging new frontiers. New frontiers include, among other things, the certainty of sharing of intelligent information that would be available to both the agent and the principal in the context of the agency theory.
- The advantages of intelligent systems are updateability and connectivity. Using these strengths, we think intelligent agents will be swift in picking up the information discrepancies. Intelligent systems have the capability of harvesting information from different sources. Once gathered, this information will be updated in the principal's system, as the systems will be integrated.
- It is probable that with the knowledge that intelligent agents are deployed widely and that these intelligent systems have the capability of harvesting data from different repositories, the agent will moderate his or her behaviour to be closely aligned with that of the principal.
- AI could bring about moderated behaviour to agents. This moderated behaviour is likely to be aligned to the principal's expectation.

References

Agrawal A, Gans J, Goldfarb A (2018) Prediction machines: the simple economics of artificial intelligence. Harvard Business Review Press, Boston, MA

Eisenhardt MK (1989) Agency theory: an assessment and review. Academy of management review. Sage, London

Harari YN (2018) 21 Lessons for the 21st century. Jonathan Cape, London

ICAEW. (2005). Audit quality: agency theory and the role of audit. https://www.icaew.com//media/corporate/files/technical/audit-and-assurance/audit-quality/audit-qualityforum/agency-theory-and-the-role-of-audit.ashx/. Accessed 23 Dec 2015

Jensen MC, Meckling WH (1976) Theory of the firm: managerial behaviour, agency costs and ownership structure. J Financ Econ 3:305–360

Kaplan Publishing (2018) Kaplan Financial Knowledge Bank. http://kfknowledgebank.kaplan.co.uk/KFKB/Wiki%20Pages/NonFinancial%20Performance%20Indicators%20%28NFPIs%29.aspx. Accessed 12 Dec 2019

Kopp C (2019) Agency theory investopedia. https://www.investopedia.com/terms/a/agencytheory.asp. Accessed 23 Dec 2019

Linder S, Foss NJ (2015) Agency theory; International encyclopaedia of social and behavioural sciences, 2nd edn. https://www.coursehero.com/file/30959452/08-Linder-Foss-2015-Agency-Theory-Elsevier-Encyclopedia-of-Social-Sciencespdf/. Accessed 26 Dec 2019

Marwala T, Hurwitz E (2017) Artificial intelligence and economic theory: skynet in the market. Springer. ISBN: 978-3-319-66103-2

Mitnick BM (2006) Origin of the theory of agency: an account by one of the theory's originators. http://www.pitt.edu/~mitnick/agencytheory/Agencytheoryindex.html/. Accessed 3 Mar 2016

Moloi T (2009) Assessment of corporate governance reporting in the annual report of South African listed companies. Masters dissertation, University of South Africa

Panda B, Leepsa NM (2017) Agency theory: review of theory and evidence on problems and perspectives. Indian J Corp Gov 10(1):74–95

Teeboom L (2018) The agency theory in financial management. Retrieved from Houston Chronicle https://smallbusiness.chron.com/agency-theory-financial-management-81899.html

Tiessen P, Waterhouse JH (1983) Towards a descriptive theory of management accounting. J Account 3:251–267

Chapter 12
The Legitimacy Theory and the Legitimacy Gap

12.1 Introduction

It is apparent that in order to sustain legitimacy, one of the most important pillars is disclosure of information by organizations. The challenge is that it is organizations that decide which information to disclose and which one not to. We think this is one of the key causes of the legitimacy gap. Legitimacy gap is basically a change that is a result of the appearance of information that was not previously known about the organization (Islam 2017). We think this is information asymmetry in the context of the legitimacy theory, which is our focus in explaining the role of AI. In essence, we examine the role AI plays in moderating the legitimacy gap emanating from information asymmetry. In order to contextualize our objective, we first provide a broader discussion of the legitimacy theory.

According to Guthrie et al. (2006), the legitimacy theory is derived from the concept of organizational legitimacy. This implies that organizations seek to be perceived by stakeholders as legitimate. The concept of legitimacy has been defined by Dowling and Pfeffer (1975: 122) "as a condition or status which exists when an entity's value system is congruent with the value system of the more extensive social system of which the entity is a part. When a disparity, actual or potential, exists between the two value systems, there is a threat to the entity's legitimacy".

Legitimacy is considered by Suchman (1995) as a generalized perception that the actions of an organization are desirable and appropriate within some socially constructed system of norms, values, beliefs, and definitions. Mousa and Hassan (2015) view legitimacy as "the appraisal of action in terms of shared or common values in the context of the involvement of the action in the society". Therefore, the concept of legitimacy is essential in analysing the relationships between companies and their environment (Islam 2017).

Essentially, legitimacy is about a social agreement entered into by the two parties, namely, the organization and the society. It will contain a set of indirect or straightforward assumptions by members of the society as to how the organization is expected

T. Moloi and T. Marwala, *Artificial Intelligence in Economics and Finance Theories*, Advanced Information and Knowledge Processing,
https://doi.org/10.1007/978-3-030-42962-1_12

to operate (Abreu 2015). On the basis that there is a socially constructed system of norms, values, beliefs and definitions to which the organization is expected to conduct itself, Guthrie et al. (2006) posit that the legitimacy theory states that business organizations continually seek to make sure that they operate within what they are obligated, including norms of their respective societies.

According to Hassaan (2016), societies are different. Suppose you are in a country like South Africa, there are different tribal groups as well as different classes of society. In such a diverse society, Hassaan (2016) points out, the legitimacy theory seeks to void the divergent group and interests that exist in a society. In essence, Hassaan's (2016) argument is that the legitimacy theory does not take into consideration that legitimacy would be interpreted differently from one society to another. Often, the interpretation relies on societal values, political systems and official ideology.

For Islam (2017), the legitimacy theory has its basis in the theoretical paradigm of the political economy. This suggests that the economic domain may not be regarded in separation from the political, social and institutional framework in which the economy is positioned (Islam 2017).

According to Zyznarska-Dworczak (2017), there are reasons the legitimacy theory is important. These are briefly outlined thus:

- The legitimacy theory assists in understanding the organization's behaviour in implementing, developing and communicating its social contract, which eventually enables the recognition of its objectives.
- The legitimacy theory is crucial in explaining the organization's behaviour in implementing and developing social responsibility policies and then communicating results.
- It treats corporate social and environmental performance and disclosure of this information as ways to fulfil the organization's social contract, which enables the recognition of its objectives.
- The legitimacy theory has a wealthy disciplinary background based on management theory, institutional theory and stakeholder theory, and therefore, it is used in many scientific studies, as well as by accounting researchers.
- The dominant status that legitimacy theory has attained in social accounting research has contributed to the understanding of the motives and the incentives that lead firms' managers to engage in social and environmental disclosure activities (Archel et al. 2009).

12.2 Legitimacy Theory and the Social Contract

Zyznarska-Dworczak (2017) views the legitimacy theory as "concerned with the broader stakeholders and not only the society in which the organization operates". Accordingly, the legitimacy theory spells out that the continued existence of an organization is established both by market strength and social expectations. This description demonstrates that markets also have a role in crafting the rules of engagement.

In order for the organization to be successful in winning favour with its stakeholders, it needs to have an understating of the broader concerns of the public. This will often be articulated in community expectations, and it becomes an essential prerequisite for an organization's survival. In this regard, Zyznarska-Dworczak (2017) points out that the legitimacy theory focuses on the supposition that an organization must keep its social position by responding to society's requirements and providing society what it wants.

For Burlea and Popa (2013), the legitimacy theory is viewed as "a mechanism that supports organization in implementing and developing voluntary social and environmental disclosures in order to fulfil their social contract". Shocker and Sethi (1973: 67) describe the social contract as applicable to any social institution and business that operates within society. Social institutions and businesses will operate in the society through a social contract. The contract between the organization and the society could be expressed or implied. The survival and growth of this social institution and business will be based on the delivery of some socially desirable ends to society in general, and the distribution of economic, social or political benefits to groups from which that particular social institution and business derive power.

The existence of the social contract between society and the organization provides a mechanism for the recognition of the organization. This existence of this contract becomes vital for the survival of an organization, particularly during turbulent times.

According to Das (2016), the legitimacy theory highlights the extent to which corporate social and environmental disclosures are influenced by the boundaries established by the society in order to be appreciated and avoid being viewed in a negative light by the community in which the company operates. In adopting the legitimacy theory, organizations will voluntarily make available information through reports on activities that management perceives as necessary to communities (Guthrie et al. 2006).

Burlea and Popa (2013) warn that organizations should avoid a situation where they are perceived by society as not being concerned about its norms, standards and values. Failure to respect the moral values of the society in which the organization operates could lead to disturbances to organizational activities by society. These disturbances may even lead to the failure of the organization (Burlea and Popa 2013). What we learn from Burlea and Popa's (2013) warning is that the organization must justify its existence through legitimate economic and social actions that do not threaten the existence of the society in which it operates.

Since the legitimacy theory hinges on the impression that there must be a social agreement between an organization and the community where it operates, and it then follows that the society will have a role of some sort in whether or not the operations of a company continue to be successful (Branco and Rodrigues 2006; Mohammed 2018). Without the society lending legitimacy to an organization operating in its space, Branco and Rodrigues (2006) assert, it will be difficult for such an organization to maintain the interests of stakeholders (Branco and Rodrigues 2006). In view of the role that society has on the potential success of an organization, O'Donovan (2000) concludes that a legitimate organization will be described as the one whose actions must be perceived by members of society as being congruent with socially constructed systems of norms, values and beliefs.

12.3 Legitimacy Theory and Disclosures

Companies would voluntarily report on activities as they continually seek to ensure that they operate within the bounds and norms of their respective societies. More and more, it is becoming apparent that society has a considerable role in the continuing existence of an organization. The society's role, as discussed in the preceding section, is that of lending legitimacy to organizations operating in their midst. As such, in order for an organization to be a going concern, it needs to pass the test of legitimacy. Abreu (2015) concurs with this. In Abreau's (2015) view, the perpetuity of an organization may be jeopardized if the society learns that an organization has violated its social agreement (Abreu 2015).

Ordinarily, society is not part of the internal machinery of an organization. Therefore, society relies on reports that are generated by the organization for its information about the organization. In cases where organizational operations are such that they involve the production of goods, for instance, mining and quarrying, forestry and fisheries, the society will be able to receive signals based on operational behaviour. In addition to the monitoring by authorities, the community and in some cases non-governmental organizations, the information contained in the social and environmental disclosures of the corporate reports indicate whether an organization adheres to the notion of legitimacy theory.

According to Mousa and Hassan (2015), organizations that seek to gain, maintain or repair their legitimacy will utilize social and environmental disclosures to communicate with these stakeholders. There has been a rise in the disclosures of societal information on corporate reports. Guthrie et al. (2006) have attributed this increase in organizations' disclosures of societal and environmental information to the legitimacy theory.

According to Seckin-Celik (2017), the increase in disclosures of societal and environmental information is attributable to events containing environmental accidents and disasters, corporate accounting scandals, economic crises and other similar issues that have raised massive criticism against companies. In concurring with this point, Das (2016) is of the view that the global financial crisis and the instability of the financial markets placed enormous pressure on organizations to re-evaluate their value systems and to emphasize the importance of legitimacy (Das 2016). It is apparent that the events discussed above, among other developments, have created inconceivable pressure on organizations to become transparent and accountable.

It would appear that the point both Das (2016) and Seckin-Celik (2017) are making is that these events resulted in the loss of legitimacy. Due to the fact that some of these organizations were deemed too big to fail and they were bailed out using the public purse (taxpayers' dollars), it was expected that there was to be massive criticism and pressure against these organizations. To claw back legitimacy, additional disclosures of information were required in order to promote transparency and accountability.

The point that we have made above is supported by Porter and Kramer (2011) in their concept of organizational survival. Accordingly, the organization would require legitimacy in order to continue its operations. One of the ways of gaining legitimacy is reporting on social and environmental issues. Burlea and Popa (2013) concur with this point. Their view is that the new economic, social and environmental challenges dictate that organizations and governments respect the rules, values and norms, and to voluntarily disclose social and environmental information in order to prove their compliance.

12.4 Legitimacy Gap

Legitimacy appears to be a moving target between the different parties. In essence, what we learn from Guthrie et al. (2006) is that societal expectations are not permanent; they evolve. Guthrie et al. (2006) point out that at some point in time, congruence between institutional actions and social values can be met. Guthrie et al. (2006) view is supported by Islam (2017). Accordingly, the legitimation process between different parties is a continuous target because new events or incidents that threaten organizational legitimacy can arise or past legitimacy threatening events can recur.

The fact that legitimacy is a moving target means that the organization has to the pragmatic. According to Guthrie et al. (2006), organizations are seen as pragmatic if they are responsive to the environment in which they operate. They further need to make disclosures in order to demonstrate that they are also adapting to the dynamism of the environment in which they find themselves.

Now, the changes in the environment in which organizations find themselves would create a shift in expectations. Guthrie et al. (2006) proposed that such a change brings a shift to legitimacy, and this shift creates a "legitimacy gap". The concept of legitimacy gap is seen by Lindblom (1994) as "the difference between the expectations of the relevant stakeholders relating to how an organization should act, and how the organization does act". According to Islam (2017), a legitimacy gap is based on relational perception, which accepts a relationship among organizations and society.

Figure 12.1 demonstrates the legitimacy gap.

Figure 12.1 graphically depicts the concept of the legitimacy gap. As discussed above, legitimacy gap refers to "the difference between the expectations of the relevant stakeholders relating to how an organization should act, and how the organization does act". We think the legitimacy gap will be demonstrated by the arrow that points to the space between the curve that demonstrates the changing expectations, while the organizational actions remain constant.

Islam (2017) suggests that there are two primary sources of legitimacy gaps, which are described thus:

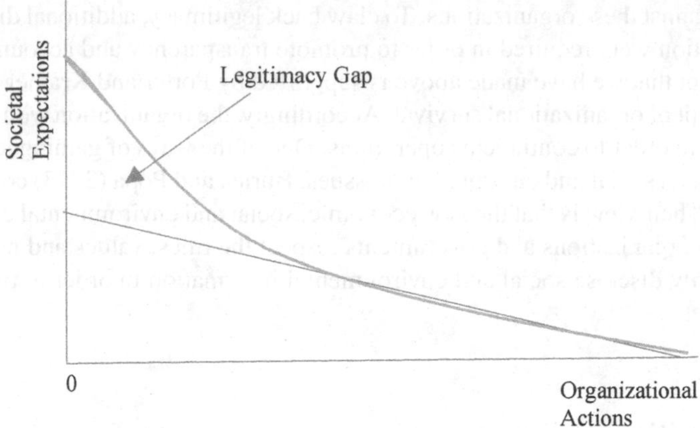

Fig. 12.1 Graphical presentation of legitimacy gap

- The changes in societal expectation—this causes a shift from what is expected from the organization to what it can actually deliver. In this regard, Islam (2017) indicates that "societal expectations would have changed, which leads to a gap". A gap arises because the organization's practice has not changed.
- Information asymmetry—this is a change that is a result of the appearance of information that was not previously known about the organization (Islam 2017).

Nasi et al. (1997) refer to a change that is a result of the appearance of information that was not previously known about the organization as organizational shadows. Accordingly, Nasi et al. (1997) submit that "the potential body of information about the corporation that is unavailable to the public stands as a constant potential threat to a corporation's legitimacy. When part of the organizational shadow is revealed, either accidentally or through the activities of an activist group or a journalist, a legitimacy gap may be created".

As such, it can be expected that this piece of information that would not have been available to the public becomes a ticking time bomb to the reputation of the organization. It puts the organization's legitimacy at stake. As mitigation, Lindblom (1994) suggests that a legitimacy gap comes with a threat to the organization's legitimacy and therefore needs to be addressed accordingly.

According to Islam (2017), an organization has to put strategies in place to deal with the legitimacy gap. Organizations that do not have legitimacy strategies in place will be vulnerable, and this will be exacerbated should threats arise. Fiedler and Deegan (2002) suggest that such strategies may include targeted disclosures and collaborating with other entities that, in themselves, are considered to be legitimate.

According to Lindblom (1994), there are four paths of action that an organization can follow in order to maintain legitimacy. The organization can seek to:

- Educate and inform its relevant stakeholders about actual changes in the organization's performance and activities;

- Change the perceptions of the relevant publics but not change its actual behaviour;
- Manipulate perceptions by deflecting attention from the issue of concern to other related issues; and
- Change external expectations of its performance.

What does this mean in practice? Mousa and Hassan (2015: 43) outline the practical steps of the four paths of actions suggested by Lindblom (1994). These are below:

- The organization can adapt its output, goals and methods of operation to conform to prevailing definitions of legitimacy.
- An organization can attempt, through communication, to alter the definition of social legitimacy so that it conforms to the organization's present practices, output and values.
- Organizations can attempt, through communication, to become identified with symbols, values or institutions which have a strong base of legitimacy.
- Companies may seek to achieve legitimacy by appearing to be doing the right things or not be involved in doing the wrong things when this appearance may have little in common with the company's actual environmental performance.

In O'Donovan's (2002) view, the moment legitimacy is threatened, an organization will embark on a process of legitimation that is targeted at those groups that it perceives to be its "conferring public". This calls for an organization to really engage itself in managing legitimacy issues. Islam (2017) advises that managing legitimacy effectively requires the organization to consider the following factors:

- Identifying its conferring publics;
- Establishing its conferring publics' social and environmental values and perception of the corporation's public pressure variables;
- Deciding on the purpose of any potential organizational response to legitimacy threats; and
- Deciding on what tactics and disclosure options are available and suitable for managing legitimacy related to the purpose of the organizational response (Islam 2017).

Since the legitimacy theory is considered a vital resource on which an organization depends for survival, an organization will pursue strategies to ensure its continued survival (Mousa and Hassan 2015). Organizations will need to carefully manage their conduct and the perceptions that society has about it.

Cormier and Gordon (2001) remind us that legitimacy is based on perceptions, should the bomb explode, the organization concerned will have to formulate the remedial actions. In order for remedial action to affect external parties, they must address the core issues. Further, these remedial actions must be accompanied by publicized disclosure. Consequently, Deegan (2002) states that it becomes essential to manage this process through publicized corporate disclosures and other publicly released documents.

12.5 Artificial Intelligence and the Legitimacy Gap

During the discussions, we indicated that Seckin-Celik (2017) argued that the increase in disclosures of societal and environmental information could be attributed to events containing environmental accidents and disasters, corporate accounting scandals, economic crises and other similar issues that have raised massive criticism against companies. We observed that Das (2016) concurred and was of the view that the global financial crisis and the instability of the financial markets placed enormous pressure on organizations to re-evaluate their values systems and to emphasize the importance of legitimacy. Our approach was that these events, among other developments, have created inconceivable pressure on organizations to become transparent and accountable.

On the basis of this, it is clear that in order to sustain legitimacy, one of the most important pillars is disclosures of information by organizations. The challenge is that it is organizations that decide which information to disclose and which one not to. We think this is one of the critical causes of the legitimacy gap. Legitimacy gap is a change that is a result of the appearance of information that was not previously known about the organization (Islam 2017). We think this is information asymmetry in the context of the legitimacy theory, which is our focus in explaining the role of AI. In essence, we examine the role AI plays in moderating the legitimacy gap emanating from information asymmetry.

The fourth industrial revolution is a data-driven era, characterized by intense digitization and automation. The advent of machine learning means that data that would have been deemed irrelevant could now be found useful. Economic agents are expected to harvest and store this data with the hope that, once analysed through AI-powered models, it could explain phenomena previously deemed obscure.

One of the advantages of intelligent agents is their updateability and connectivity (Harari 2018). In the context of harvested and stored large data sets, intelligent agents linked (connected) to the data repositories would be updated on an ongoing basis as the new data is being captured or it becomes available through unstructured sources. This data would previously have been difficult to collate. Social media and other sources would make it possible to harvest this data.

Once harvested, AI-powered models will analyse it, which will assist organizations in predicting expectations. Perhaps authorities could deploy the same technology on behalf of societies that are unable to, in order to reduce the information gap between the organization and the society.

Again, we draw a similar conclusion as in the previous chapters on matters relating to the information asymmetry. We reiterate our view that that AI brings the possibility of building, linking and analysing big data sets that would otherwise be impossible for a human being. This is because intelligent machines can process vast amounts of data, whether in a structured or unstructured format.

The Institute of Chartered Accountants of England and Wales (2018) has argued that intelligent machines could process this data far much more than humans ever would. What makes intelligent machines more suitable for the purpose of dealing with information asymmetry and reducing the legitimacy gap is the fact that they can pick up weaker or more complex patterns in data than we can (The Institute of Chartered Accountants of England and Wales 2018).

As suggested by the Institute, intelligent machines may be better in environments that we find less predictable, such as the shift in expectations, and they pick up data that we would otherwise have ignored because of their ability to pick up weaker or more complex patterns in data.

12.6 Key Points

- In order to sustain legitimacy, one of the most important pillars is disclosure of information by organizations. The challenge is that it is organizations that decide which information to disclose and which one not to. We think this is one of the critical reasons for the legitimacy gap.
- Legitimacy gap is basically a change that is a result of the appearance of information that was not previously known about the organization.
- The fourth industrial revolution is a data-driven era, characterized by intense digitization and automation. The advent of machine learning means that data that would have been deemed irrelevant could now be found useful. Economic agents are expected to harvest and store this data with the hope that once analysed through AI-powered models, it could explain phenomena previously deemed obscure.
- Intelligent machines can process vast amounts of data, whether in a structured or unstructured format.
- The ability of intelligent machines to pick up weaker or more complex patterns in data than we can make them more suitable for dealing with information asymmetry and reducing the legitimacy gap.
- Intelligent machines may be better in environments that we find less predictable, such as the shift in expectations or picking up data that we would otherwise have ignored because of their ability to pick up weaker or more complex patterns in data.

References

Abreu R (2015) From legitimacy to accounting and auditing for citizenship. Procedia Econ Finance 23:665–670

Archel P, Husillos J, Larrinaga C, Spence C (2009) Social disclosure, legitimacy theory and the role of the state. Account Audit Account J 22(8):1284–1307

Branco MC, Rodrigues LL (2006) Communication of corporate social responsibility by Portuguese banks: a legitimacy theory perspective. Corp Commun Int J 11(3):232–248

Burlea ŞA, Popa I (2013) Legitimacy theory. In: Idowu SO, Capaldi N, Zu L, das Gupta A (eds) Encyclopedia of corporate social responsibility. Springer, Berlin, Heidelberg, pp 1579–1584

Cormier D, Gordon I (2001) An examination of social and environmental reporting strategies. Account Audit Account J 14(5):587–616

Das RC (2016) Handbook of research on global indicators of economic and political convergence. Katwa College, India

Deegan C (2002) The legitimizing effect of social and environmental disclosures—a theoretical foundation. Account Audit Account J 15(3):282–311

Dowling J, Pfeffer J (1975) Organizational legitimacy: social values and organizational behaviour. Pac Sociol Rev 18:122–136

Fiedler T, Deegan C (2002) Environmental collaborations within the building and construction industry: a consideration of the motivations to collaborate. In: Proceedings of the critical perspectives on accounting conference, New York. http://aux.zicklin.baruch.cuny.edu/critical/html2/8036deegan.html

Guthrie J, Cuganeson S, Ward L (2006) Legitimacy theory: a story of reporting social and environmental matters within the Australian food and beverage industry. The University of Sydney, 5th Asian Pacific Interdisciplinary Research in Accounting (APIRA) Conference, 8–10 July 2007, Auckland, New Zealand. https://papers.ssrn.com/sol3/papers.cfm?abstract_id=1360518. Accessed 13 Aug 2018

Harari YN (2018) 21 Lessons for the 21st century. Jonathan Cape, London

Hassaan, M. (2016). Handbook of research on global indicators of economic and political convergence. Katwa College, India. https://books.google.co.zw/books?hl=en&lr=&id=NLnLDAAAQBAJ&oi=fnd&pg=PR1&dq=Hassaan,+M.+(2016).+Handbook+of+Research+on+Global+Indicators+of+Economic+and+Political+Convergence.+Katwa+College,+&ots=HJjm8sGQoz&sig=DAf7W8bcBo_aOotE4i6PkLw0YQw&redir_esc=y#v=onepage&q&f=false. Accessed 24 Dec 2019

Islam MA (2017) CSR reporting and legitimacy theory: some thoughts on future research agenda. In: Aluchna M, Idowu SO (eds) The dynamics of corporate social responsibility: a critical approach to theory and practice, pp 323–339. https://papers.ssrn.com/sol3/papers.cfm?abstract_id=2947527

Lindblom C (1994) The implications of organizational legitimacy for corporate social performance and disclosure. Critical Perspectives on Accounting Conference, New York, NY

Mohammed SD (2018) Mandatory social and environmental disclosure: a performance evaluation of listed Nigerian oil and gas companies pre- and post-mandatory disclosure requirements. J Finance Account 6(2):56–68

Mousa GA, Hassan NT (2015) Legitimacy theory and environmental practices: short notes. Int J Bus Stat Anal 2(1):41–53

Nasi T, Nasi S, Phillips N, Zyglidopoulos S (1997) The evolution of corporate social responsiveness: an exploratory study of finnish and Canadian forestry companies. Bus Soc 38(3):296–321

O'Donovan G (2000) Legitimacy theory as an explanation for corporate environmental disclosures. Thesis, Victoria University of Technology, Melbourne, Australia

O'Donovan G (2002) Environmental disclosures in the annual report: extending the applicability and predictive power of legitimacy theory. Account Audit Account J 15(3):344–71

Porter ME, Kramer MR (2011) How to reinvent capitalism and unleash a wave of innovation and growth. The big idea, creating shared value. http://www.coherence360.com/praxis/wp-content/uploads/2015/08/Michael_Porter_Creating_Shared_Value.pdf. Accessed 23 Dec 2019

Seckin-Celik T (2017) Sustainability reporting and sustainability in the Turkish business context: in ethics. https://www.igi-global.com/chapter/sustainability-reporting-and-sustainability-in-the-turkish-business-context/173942. Accessed 23 Dec 2019

Shocker AD, Sethi SP (1973) An approach to developing societal preferences in developing corporate action strategies. Calif Manag Rev 14(4):97–105

Suchman MC (1995) Managing legitimacy: strategic and institutional approaches. Acad Manag Rev 20(3):571–610

The Institute of Chartered Accountants of England and Wales (2018) Artificial intelligence and the future of accountancy. ICAEW Thought Leadership, IT Faculty, UK

Zyznarska-Dworczak B (2017) Legitimacy theory in management accounting research. Problemy ZarzÈdzania 16(1):195–203

Chapter 13
Synopsis: Artificial Intelligence in Economics and Finance Theories

13.1 Introduction

In Chap. 1, we submitted that the world is changing rapidly. We pointed out that there is no other time in history when virtually every aspect, whether it is human life, economies or politics, among other things, has been affected the rapid change brought by developments in information technology (Harari 2018). We observed that technological advances have allowed humanity to discover powerful energy sources, discover faster modes of transportation for humans, goods and services, improved the speed in which we communicate, landed human beings on the moon, and there is even an attempt to send a mission to the sun.

We further observed that technology has allowed human beings to have a better mode of diagnosing and even curing diseases. We made the point that agricultural yields have also seen an improvement, thanks to technological advances. In a sense, advances in technology have enabled humanity to conquer the barriers of nature. We argued that due to technology, life has certainly improved compared to our ancestors.

In discussing the industrial revolutions, we made the point that it is clear that each of them has had a unique impact on every aspect of human life, including business. What was of interest to us, though, was that literature has not attempted to utilize these advances in technology in order to modernize economics and finance theories that are fundamental in the decision-making process. We argued that economics and finance theories are fundamental to allocating scarce resources and several other things.

We accepted the view that "with the simulated intelligence in machines, which allows machines to act like humans and to some extent even anticipate events better than humans, thanks to their ability to handle massive data sets", economics and finance theories needed to be attended to one more time. However, this time it will be the meaning of these theories "in the context of the agent wanting to make a decision that will be under scrutiny".

We concurred with the view that nowadays, AI is everywhere. Agrawal et al. (2018) point out that AI is in "our phones, cars, shopping experiences, romantic

T. Moloi and T. Marwala, *Artificial Intelligence in Economics and Finance Theories*, Advanced Information and Knowledge Processing,
https://doi.org/10.1007/978-3-030-42962-1_13

matchmaking, hospitals, banks and all over in the media". We further reviewed some of the definitions of artificial intelligence. In our review, we observed that AI is a technique that is used to make computers intelligent (Marwala 2007, 2009). There are three types of artificial intelligence, and these are machine learning, computational intelligence and soft computing (Marwala 2009). Computational intelligence is the use of intelligent biological systems such as the flocking of birds or the colony of ants to build intelligent economies. Computational intelligence has been used successfully to create systems such as Google Maps that identify the shortest distances between two points (Marwala 2012).

Based on the review of related literature, we point out that it has been established that artificial intelligence can be used effectively as a prediction tool. Given this, we pointed out that in their attempt to clear future uncertainties so that sound decisions can be made, agents use predictions as an input into the decision-making process. In this regard, economics and finance theories would have provided a framework in which agents make these decisions on how to allocate scarce resources (Marwala 2013, 2014, 2015).

We acknowledged that as "AI seizes all aspects of human life, there is a fundamental shift in the way in which humans are thinking of and doing things" (Harari 2018). We further accepted that under ordinary circumstances, "humans have relied on economics and finance theories to make sense of, and predict concepts such as comparative advantage, long-run economic growth, lack or distortion of information and failures, role of labour as a factor of production and the decision-making process for the purpose of allocating resources among other theories".

We pointed out that the main feature of these theories is that they attempt to eliminate the effects of uncertainties by attempting to bring the future to the present. The fundamentals of this statement are deeply rooted in risk and risk management. The International Standardisation Organisation (ISO), in standard number 310,00, defines risk as "the effect of uncertainty on the objective". In other words, uncertainties are the main component of the deviations from the expected outcomes (Moloi 2016).

13.2 Synopsis of Theories Examined

In **Chap**. 1, we pointed out that in behavioural sciences, economics as a discipline has always provided a well-established foundation for understanding uncertainties and what this means for decision-making (Agrawal et al. 2018). We noted that economics had done this through different models that attempt to predict the future. On its part, we acknowledged that risk management attempts to hedge or mitigate these uncertainties in order for "the planner" to reach a favourable outcome.

We reiterate our view that the main feature of economic theories is that they try to eliminate the effects of uncertainties by attempting to bring the future to the present. Agrawal et al. (2018) have argued that AI (at least as it is right now) "does not bring us intelligence, but a critical component of intelligence-prediction". This is what economics and financial theories have been deployed to do by humans in the past.

We hypothesized that with AI providing us with a critical component of intelligence, how economics and finance theories have been presented would be impacted. We provide a summary of the book chapters that focuses on how artificial intelligence is to redefine specific relevant economic and financial theories, which for many years, have specifically been used to eliminate uncertainties to allow agents to make informed decisions.

Chapter 2 of our book introduced the growth model, which was followed by the examination of the tenets of this theory, such as the catching up growth phenomenon, the steady growth path phenomenon and the cutting edge growth path phenomenon. In this chapter, we introduced two scenarios that seek to explain how AI could affect the growth model as we understand it. In the era of artificial intelligence, where a considerable part of the production line will be automated, the assumptions of the Solow growth theory are affected.

In our assessment, there exist two scenarios that could play out. In an environment characterized by intense automation, the first scenario could see a situation where classifications are left as they are in this theory. This scenario will see the robotic infrastructure or automation programs replace part of or all labour. This will result in a situation where theory is revised to indicate that the amount that each robotic infrastructure or a computer program produces in the economy will be dependent on allocated capital per robot (and/or partially labour).

The second scenario could include a condition where the robotic infrastructure or computer program is treated as part of the capital. In these conditions, the straight-line curve that illustrates the depreciation curve will be steeper. In this scenario, since total/partial labour will be out of work, it will not be in a position to save, pay taxes or demand goods that will massively be produced by the automated manufacturing factories. In this scenario, since there are no excess funds to preserve, investments to the new capital infrastructure will shrink.

The levels of investment will be lower than the depreciation required even to maintain the existing infrastructure. In this regard, the expectation is that no new capital infrastructure will be undertaken. Thus, the output per robotic support will eventually decline. If these scenarios play themselves out, the long-run steady state is replaced by the long-run economic crisis.

Chapter 3 introduced David Ricardo's theory, which is sometimes known as the Ricardian Model of comparative advantage. Primarily, we intended to examine its underlying assumptions. We did this to lay the ground for understanding the critical pillars of the model. We observe that, in essence, the Ricardian Model assumed two countries, producing two goods that are homogeneous across countries and firms within an industry. In this theory, labour is the main factor of production, mobile within the country's industries but cannot move abroad. Labour is further homogeneous within a country; however, this may be different across countries.

The implication of homogeneous labour within a country with differences between countries implies that the production technology could be different between the two trading nations. Technological advances have turned the world into a global village.

In essence, the borders have virtually flattened. We determine that AI will change the very nature of the Ricardian theory in the sense that as it evolves, it flattens the borders and possibly reduces reliance on labour. For instance, one information technology specialist can give guidance on how an application works over the Internet while based somewhere in the world, doctors can perform virtual life-saving operations, and professors can give virtual classes.

We discussed the dual-sector model in **Chap**. 4. Our primary aim was the determination of the impact of AI on this. In reviewing the literature on the dual-sector model, what is clear is that labour is the crucial factor of production in both the agricultural sector and the industrial sector. It is common cause that in the era that is characterized by technological advances, particularly AI in workplaces, we are beginning to observe considerable parts of the production line taking the automated forms. We think that in areas where it has not, those areas that involve repetitive tasks, the expectation is that automation would happen. This affects the critical aspect of the dual-sector model, which is labour.

From the perspective of automated agents, the idea that labour can easily migrate from the sector that is characterized by low levels of education to the industrial sector will falter. Firstly, if we were to suppose, as does Lewis, that the industrial sector will be highly capitalized and that profits are reinvested in order to generate efficiencies, it is given that this is a sector that will take advantage of machines' efficiencies, and automate.

As such, with AI-powered agents such as robots, there may not be employment opportunities in the destiny sector of the economy as Arthur Lewis espoused. Expectations are that factories and the industrial sector will be lean, specialised and consisting of highly skilled human resources that will be working together with machines. Therefore, with leaner factories and the demand for highly skilled resources, there will not be migration between sectors.

AI-powered machines are already deployed in the agricultural sector in order to improve yields. The agricultural sector itself, in the era dominated by AI, is not a feeder to the industrial sector but a fully fledged sector that will also be leaner with machines, having a more significant role to play. So, labour could also be expected to get a squeeze on this front as the sector moves to become highly capitalized and profits are being reinvested in order to generate efficiencies.

In **Chap**. 5, we discussed the dynamic inconsistency theory, which reflects a changing nature of economic agents' preference over a while, which could result in these preferences differing at some point in the preference continuum, yielding inconsistencies. This means that not all selected preferences are aligned and that there is a misalignment somewhere in the preference continuum.

In our observation, we point out that one of the reasons there is a shift from the original pre-commitment is the fact that time presents economic agents with many options that they may not have considered when making decisions in T_0, given the information at their disposal. For these reasons, we think dynamic inconsistency occurs because of the existence of imperfect information.

In recent times that are characterized by prominent utilization of artificial intelligence, and where we realize the emergence of large databases that store structured and unstructured data, our view is that the presence of AI-powered analytics will moderate inconsistencies. Using their strength, which lies in these two characteristics, we think intelligent agents will be swift in assisting the economic agents in harvesting information from different sources. Once gathered, this information will be analysed, which will reduce uncertainties, thus providing the agent with various options.

With their ability to store the information, learn about the previous behaviour of the agent and possibly pre-empt the next move that the agent is likely to take, while also providing the basket of options, we also think that AI would awaken the subconscious mind of the agent, challenging the notion of dynamic inconsistency with that of an informed choice. Our conclusion then is that AI will provide economic agents with a powerful tool that will allow them to make predictions with a certain degree of accuracy, thus moderating the dynamic inconsistencies.

Chapter 6 examined the Philipps Curve. This theory states that inflation and unemployment have a stable and inverse relationship (Phillips 1958). In this theory, economic growth is expected to generate inflation and more work opportunities, which decreases unemployment. We review how the application of AI would impact assumptions of the Philips Curve as well as the potential impact of AI on this theory. In particular, our focus is on the critical aspect of the Philips Curve which is unemployment and inflation. When the Phillips Curve made an appearance into the scene, labour had a considerable role in the production of goods and services.

With several countries intensely pursuing technology, we begin to see most factories adopting AI-powered technologies in their production lines. Mostly, we are beginning to see a massive line of production processes being automated. When a considerable part of the production line becomes automated (mechanized), we think the critical aspect of the Philips Curve will be impacted. Both inflation and unemployment variables are key to the Phillips Curve.

We conclude that in the era of artificial intelligence, where a considerable part of the production line is expected to be automated (mechanized), the critical aspect of the Philips Curve will be impacted. In the automated world, economic growth could be fuelled by robotic infrastructure. Because the robotic infrastructure would have possibly replaced individuals, growth would not be accompanied by employment opportunities. At the same time, since this could result in unemployment, the demand for goods and services could be expected to be put under pressure. If supply remains the same because the robotic infrastructure will be producing potentially at a higher rate than humans, prices could be expected to decline, dampening inflation prospects.

In **Chap**. 7, we discussed the Laffer Curve. We looked at the effect of AI on the Curve. We noted that Arthur Laffer advanced an argument that changes in tax rates affect government revenues differently in the short term and an extended basis. Initially, the increase in the tax rate will be followed by an increase in tax revenues generated by the government. This will continue until it reaches the prohibitive point. Beyond the prohibitive point, additional taxes result in reduced government revenue. If this continues, the curve shows that government revenue would decline until the point of zero, where the government would generate no revenue. The introduction of intelligent machines such as the robotic infrastructure, consisting of AI, to perform tasks that are performed by human beings neutralizes the Laffer Curve.

It is apparent that the Laffer Curve was not designed to deal with such a development. With AI, no matter how many movements are in the personal income tax rate, until the government introduces taxes, say on computerized robots, it will not derive the revenue it was deriving prior to the introduction of intelligent machines. This poses a challenge to the theory. In the case of corporate tax, we are of the view that the introduction of AI does not have much effect. The tenets of the theory will still hold.

Chapter 8 discussed the concept of adverse selection, which is a problem that stems from information asymmetry. Information asymmetry is where a strategic behaviour by the more informed party in a contract works against the interest of the less informed counterparties. We looked at the two ways in which management literature has suggested for managing this, both in the accounting framework and the agency theory.

We observe that in the agency theory, individual scholars have suggested that there should be penalties or incentives so that transparent behaviour is promoted to limit the agency problem. Our conclusion in this regard is that the action of whether to disclose material facts or not is still dependent on one economic agent, which is expected to be unlikely in a situation where the disclosure of such information has the potential to reduce economic benefits to that particular economic agent.

On the IAS conceptual framework, we observe that it appears to be appealing to the conscience or ethics that economic agents should do what is morally correct, which is clear from the use of the word "fair". The challenge of this approach is whether the economic agent could be persuaded to do what is fair in the face of potential economic losses should they cede certain strategic advantages associated with having certain information that counterparties in the transaction do not have.

The era of intense automation and digitization is likely going to push economic agents to some new forms of relationships. This could include sharing certain information that opens the opportunity for harvesting and storing big data that could be useful to economic agents. AI brings the possibility of building, linking and analysing the new big data sets that would otherwise be impossible for a human being, thus reducing the extent of adverse selection.

Chapter 9 discussed the moral hazard. We made a point that it is a concept that cannot be separated from the adverse selection, which is a problem that stems from information asymmetry. Again, we looked at the two ways in which management literature has suggested to manage asymmetric information, adverse selection and moral hazard. These are both the accounting framework and agency theory.

In looking at the agency theory as a mitigating factor to the question of asymmetric information, adverse selection and moral hazard, we make a point that the theory does not resolve these problems. In our view, the reason this solution would have difficulties in mitigating asymmetric information, adverse selection, and subsequently, the question of the moral hazard lies in the fact that the decision whether to disclose material facts or not is dependent on one economic agent. If this agent is of the view that they could gain some advantage over their counterparties, in our view, it will be unlikely that there will be a disclosure of such information.

In examining the conceptual framework of accounting, we note that the IAS is asking that the economic agent should work against maximizing what he/she could potentially gain. Our view in this regard is that the IAS appears to be appealing to the conscience or ethics that economic agents should do what is morally correct.

We are of the view that AI will outperform the mitigation actions put forward by the finance and accounting literature, the agency theory and the conceptual framework. With AI, there is no need to rely on economic agents to be "fair by disclosing material information". There is also no need to persuade economic agents by incentives of disclosing material information or coercing them with threats of penalties.

In **Chap**. 10, we discussed the creative destruction theory. The creative destruction theory was defined as the process by which information and communication technology destroys previous technological solutions and lays waste old companies in order to make room for the new companies. In recent times, searches were done through sites such as "HotBot, Ananzi Excite, WebCrawler, Ask Jeeves, Ask.com, Yahoo, Dogpile, AltaVista, Lycos, MSN Search, Bing, AOL Search, Infoseek, Go.com, Netscape, MetaCrawler" (Schwartz 2009), which have been replaced by Google, by far the largest search engine today. Large amounts of data brought about the advent of Internet of Things can mean that there are plenty of insights that companies that were affected by the gayle of destruction rarely knew existed.

Companies that are in the coalface would have had enormous data of people that use it; we think that with the AI-powered analytics, the idea of creative destruction as espoused by Schumpeter (1941), would hold as far as technology is concerned. However, companies that would be pioneers of the time may not necessarily fold and close doors. With regard to the impact of AI to the creative destruction theory, our view is that since data is the new gold, companies that take advantage of AI for the purpose of advanced data analytics would be able to deploy this for the purpose of analysing large amounts of data brought about by the advent of the Internet of Things.

Our hypothesis is that the above can only mean that there are plenty of insights for those companies in the coalface, the gayle of destruction in this regard will not bring about new entrepreneurs or new companies, but the same companies and insights from data and predictive analytics will show them which technology is to be destroyed and what it needs to be replaced with. Whatever the replacement, it will be based on troves of data, which gives these companies the competitive advantage to understand their market and where their market is headed.

Chapter 11 discussed the agency theory. The agency theory is a principle utilized in an attempt to explain the complicated relationship that exists between the owners (principal) and managers (agents) of the business. Based on this, we submit that the agency theory is an attempt to explain the complexity of human behaviour in the principal-agent relationship. We are of the view that when the desires or goals of the principal and agent conflict, it is difficult or expensive for the principal to verify what the agent is doing.

Since the theory is an attempt to explain the complexity of human behaviour in the principal-agent relationship, we pose the question; what happens to the theory in the era dominated by intelligent machines? We conclude that with AI, there will be new frontiers. New frontiers include, among other things, the certainty of intelligent sharing of information that would be available to both the agent and the principal in the context of the agency theory.

Further, we observe that the advantages of intelligent systems are updateability and connectivity. Using these strengths, we think intelligent agents will be swift in picking up information discrepancies. Intelligent systems have the capability of harvesting information from different sources. Once gathered, this information will be updated in the principal's system, as the systems will be integrated. Finally, we think it conceivable that, knowing that intelligent agents are deployed widely and that these intelligent systems have the capability of harvesting data from different repositories, perhaps the agent will moderate his or her behaviour to be closely aligned with that of the principal.

Chapter 12 discussed the legitimacy theory and legitimacy gap. We made the point that organizations seek to be perceived by stakeholders as legitimate. Because legitimacy is a moving target, organizations have to be pragmatic. The legitimacy gap will be formed due to the concept of time, which informs the movement of expectations. As time progresses, the environment in which organizations operate will shift, which would create a shift in expectations. This change brings a shift to legitimacy, and it creates a "legitimacy gap". On the basis of this, Lindblom (1994) defines the legitimacy gap as "the difference between the expectations of the relevant stakeholders relating to how an organization should act, and how the organization does act".

Mostly, two primary sources of legitimacy gap were outlined, namely, the changes in societal expectation and information asymmetry. We outlined the role of AI in moderating the legitimacy gap, specifically if the concept of information asymmetry is deemed the main driver of the gap. In the context of harvested and stored extensive data sets, we suggest that intelligent agents linked (connected) to the relevant data repositories would be updated on an ongoing basis as the new data is being captured or it becomes available through unstructured sources. This data would previously have been difficult to collate.

We point out that social media and other sources would make it possible to harvest this data. We think once harvested, AI-powered models will analyse it, which will assist organizations in predicting expectations. In cases where society is too weak, perhaps authorities could deploy the same technology on behalf of societies that are unable to, in order to, reduce the information gap between the organization and the society.

References

Agrawal A, Gans J, Goldfarb A (2018) Prediction machines: the simple economics of artificial intelligence. Harvard Business Review Press, Boston, Massachusetts

Harari YN (2018) 21 lessons for the 21st century. Jonathan Cape, London

Lindblom C (1994) The implications of organizational legitimacy for corporate social performance and disclosure. Critical Perspectives on Accounting Conference, New York, NY

Marwala T (2007) Computational intelligence for modelling complex systems. Research India Publications, Delhi

Marwala T (2009) Computational intelligence for missing data imputation, estimation, and management: knowledge optimization techniques. IGI Global, PA

Marwala T (2012) Condition monitoring using computational intelligence methods. Springer, Heidelberg

Marwala T (2013) Economic modeling using artificial intelligence methods. Springer, Heidelberg

Marwala T (2014) Artificial intelligence techniques for rational decision making. Springer, Heidelberg

Marwala T (2015) Causality, correlation, and artificial intelligence for rational decision making. World Scientific, Singapore

Moloi T (2016) A cross sectoral comparison of risk management practices in South African organizations. Probl Perspect Manag 14(3):99–106

Phillips AW (1958) The relation between unemployment and the rate of change of money wage rates in the United Kingdom, 1861–1957. Econ New Ser 25(100):283–299

Schumpeter JA (1941) An economic interpretation of our time: the lowell lectures, in the economics and sociology of capitalism. Princeton University Press, Princeton, NJ, p 349. As quoted by "Schumpeter and Regional Innovation" by Esben S Andersen. Chapter for Handbook of Regional Innovation and Growth. (ed P Cooke, Elgar Publ)

Schumpeter JA (1994) [1942] Capitalism, socialism and democracy. Harper and Brothers, New York, USA

Schwartz B (2009) A look back at the old search engines. Accessed 03 Dec 2019. https://searchengineland.com/a-look-back-at-the-old-search-engines-25766

Index

T. Moloi and T. Marwala, *Artificial Intelligence in Economics and Finance Theories*, Advanced Information and Knowledge Processing,
https://doi.org/10.1007/978-3-030-42962-1

Printed in the United States
by Baker & Taylor Publisher Services